The Cyclical Timing
of Consumer Credit, 1920-67

Philip A. Klein

The Pennsylvania State University

OCCASIONAL PAPER 113

NATIONAL BUREAU OF
ECONOMIC RESEARCH

New York 1971

Distributed by Columbia University Press

New York and London

Relation of the Directors to the Work and Publications of the National Bureau of Economic Research

1. The object of the National Bureau of Economic Research is to ascertain and to present to the public important economic facts and their interpretation in a scientific and impartial manner. The Board of Directors is charged with the responsibility of ensuring that the work of the National Bureau is carried on in strict conformity with this object.

2. The President of the National Bureau shall submit to the Board of Directors, or to its Executive Committee, for their formal adoption all specific proposals for research to be instituted.

3. No research report shall be published until the President shall have submitted to each member of the Board the manuscript proposed for publication, and such information as will, in his opinion and in the opinion of the author, serve to determine the suitability of the report for publication in accordance with the principles of the National Bureau. Each manuscript shall contain a summary drawing attention to the nature and treatment of the problem studied, the character of the data and their utilization in the report, and the main conclusions reached.

4. For each manuscript so submitted, a special committee of the Board shall be appointed by majority agreement of the President and Vice Presidents (or by the Executive Committee in case of inability to decide on the part of the President and Vice Presidents), consisting of three directors selected as nearly as may be one from each general division of the Board. The names of the special manuscript committee shall be stated to each Director when the manuscript is submitted to him. It shall be the duty of each member of the special manuscript committee to read the manuscript. If each member of the manuscript committee signifies his approval within thirty days of the transmittal of the manuscript, the report may be published. If at the end of that period any member of the manuscript committee withholds his approval, the President shall then notify each member of the Board, requesting approval or disapproval of publication, and thirty days additional shall be granted for this purpose. The manuscript shall then not be published unless at least a majority of the entire Board who shall have voted on the proposal within the time fixed for the receipt of votes shall have approved.

5. No manuscript may be published, though approved by each member of the special manuscript committee, until forty-five days have elapsed from the transmittal of the report in manuscript form. The interval is allowed for the receipt of any memorandum of dissent or reservation, together with a brief statement of his reasons, that any member may wish to express; and such memorandum of dissent or reservation shall be published with the manuscript if he so desires. Publication does not, however, imply that each member of the Board has read the manuscript, or that either members of the Board in general or the special committee have passed on its validity in every detail.

6. Publications of the National Bureau issued for informational purposes concerning the work of the Bureau and its staff, or issued to inform the public of activities of Bureau staff, and volumes issued as a result of various conferences involving the National Bureau shall contain a specific disclaimer noting that such publication has not passed through the normal review procedures required in this resolution. The Executive Committee of the Board is charged with review of all such publications from time to time to ensure that they do not take on the character of formal research reports of the National Bureau, requiring formal Board approval.

7. Unless otherwise determined by the Board or exempted by the terms of paragraph 6, a copy of this resolution shall be printed in each National Bureau publication.

(Resolution adopted October 25, 1926, and revised February 6, 1933, February 24, 1941, and April 20, 1968)

Contents

Tables

Charts

Acknowledgments

MY INTEREST in the area of consumer credit goes back a good many years and the present study has been progressing for some time on the periphery of other projects. I am aware, therefore, of obligations to many people who helped shape my view of the problems involved in the cyclical analysis of consumer credit, even though many of these individuals played no direct role in the development of the present study. More particularly, the study is a National Bureau study in methodology, in approach, and in spirit, as well as in fact. It has, therefore, like all Bureau efforts, been the recipient of much useful advice and assistance from my colleagues at the National Bureau.

Victor Zarnowitz read several drafts of the study and his constructive advice has been of great benefit to me. Likewise, I am indebted to F. Thomas Juster and Robert P. Shay for a very careful reading of the manuscript. Sophie Sakowitz was indispensable in the early stages of this study as in so many others with her help in the critical process of correctly choosing turning points in the series involved; her death was a profound loss to all of us who have relied on her at the National Bureau. Hannah Stern efficiently traced the sources of the data and Dorothy O'Brien painstakingly checked the data for the tables and charts. The study has the benefit of H. Irving Forman's expertly drawn charts and like National Bureau authors for many years I gladly acknowledge his contribution to this study. The text has been immeasurably improved by the editorial assistance of Joan Tron and Virginia Meltzer. Muriel Moeller, as always, has my great gratitude for indispensable assistance in an untold number of ways at all stages of the study. I also wish to thank Boris Shishkin, Maurice W. Lee, and Willis J. Winn of the National Bureau Board of Directors Reading Committee for their useful suggestions.

At the Pennsylvania State University I was fortunate to have a number of research assistants who helped me enormously, including James Lees Currie, Hugh Greenidge, Joseph Telep, and Leslie G. Weston. Invaluable assistance with computer programming was provided by Helen Pierce and Donna Ellenberger of the Center for Research in the College of Business Administration, and by the Pennsylvania State Computer Center. I acknowledge with gratitude the permission given by the R. L. Polk Company to utilize and publish their series dealing with New Passenger Car Registrations.

I wish also to express my appreciation to Daniel B. Suits, Julius Shiskin, and Mona B. Dingle who provided necessary advice and assistance along the way.

My greatest obligation, as is true of so many who have worked at the National Bureau in recent years, is to Geoffrey H. Moore. His keen insight, great patience, indefatigable energy, and unflagging interest helped both the study and its author far more than a few words of thanks here could possibly hope to convey.

PHILIP A. KLEIN

For Peggy

. . . consumer instalment credit is not a cyclical factor of the very first importance. Even if cyclical fluctuations in instalment credit were entirely eliminated, the business cycle would still exist. But the same could be said of many other factors and measures if each were considered in isolation. . . . But concerted action in many fields at the same time will have a noticeable stabilizing effect, and in such a system of measures the cyclical control of consumer instalment credit should find an important place.

GOTTFRIED HABERLER
Consumer Instalment Credit and Economic Fluctuations
National Bureau of Economic Research, 1942

1

Introduction

THE RAPID INCREASE in the volume of consumer credit during recent decades, both absolutely and relative to income, has attracted the interest and attention of economists concerned with the impact of this development on general economic stability. This study examines the cyclical patterns of selected measures of consumer credit activity, and analyzes their relation not only to each other but to general economic activity. The amplitudes of expansions and contractions in credit are related to comparable changes in income as one measure of the importance of credit in the economy. The major focus of the study, however, is on timing relationships—that is, on the relationships among cyclical turning points in various consumer credit series, and the relation between the credit series and general business cycles.[1]

Consumer credit can be divided broadly into instalment credit and noninstalment credit. In Chapter 2, we shall briefly consider the cyclical record of consumer credit and the contribution to that record made by both of these components. Chapter 3 then concentrates on instalment credit as the most cyclically volatile component. The impact of instalment credit on economic activity can be measured in several ways —as the volume of new credit injected into the economy (extensions), as credit paid off and thus removed from the economy (repayments), as the *change* in credit outstanding resulting from both (net credit change), or as the total amount of credit in existence at a given point in time (instalment credit outstanding). We consider the interrelationships of these four measures and their relationship to the business cycle.

---

[1] The major earlier examination of the pattern of turning points in various measures of consumer credit was Gottfried Haberler's *Consumer Instalment Credit and Economic Fluctuations* published by the National Bureau in 1942 (and dealing, therefore, exclusively with the prewar period.)

In Chapter 4, we then turn to the biggest component of instalment credit—that utilized in the purchase of automobiles. Not only is automobile instalment credit important by itself, but it can be directly related to the volume of automobiles sold. We, therefore, carry the analysis one step further—relating cycles in credit activity to cycles in the product for which the credit was created. Thus, we study the parts of consumer credit from the total to its components and, as it turns out, focus attention on that part of consumer credit most sensitive to the business cycle.

Chapter 5 lists the conclusions of the study. Appendix A is a general note on sources. Appendix B presents timing analyses utilizing new passenger car registrations as the basic reference chronology instead of the National Bureau reference dates. Appendix C contains the basic data underlying the study and brings together the relevant monthly series for 1920–67, which are nowhere else available in this form.

It is true that ultimately we are interested in the much larger question of whether movements in consumer credit reflect in general the *reaction* of this industry to prior changes in general economic activity, or whether the chain of causality is the other way round (that is, whether credit changes are part, albeit modest, of the tangled interactions that lead intermittently to recessions in the general economy), or whether the relationship is best viewed as one of mutual interaction. We trust that our study will be useful in considering this important question. It cannot possibly provide the answer by itself, partly because a study of the timing interrelationships cannot alone pose—let alone answer— all the relevant questions concerning the interrelationship of credit and other broader measures of economic activity. At the very least, one would have to consider the importance that attaches to the amplitudes of the relevant cycles and to any pattern of magnification or diminution that such analysis might reveal.

Because cyclical fluctuations do not stem primarily from consumer credit changes, our study can provide only modest evidence for the study of instability. For one thing, business cycles were a factor in economic life long before consumer credit assumed much significance. Moreover, even for products such as automobiles and other durables on which the influence of credit conditions is likely to be relatively strong, other cyclically variable factors such as price and income change are also likely to have a powerful effect on the pattern of fluctuation in expenditures.

An examination of the turning point relationships in several of the consumer credit measures, as well as in the production and sale of products for which consumer credit is used, and in general economic activity, should be of considerable benefit in helping to understand and recognize cyclical movements. To the extent that the patterns are systematic, a description of these patterns should help in knowing what to expect when examining current changes in consumer credit, and also in helping to recognize what is unusual. Increased understanding of how the credit system operates, as well as how credit variation is related to variation in purchases, can make a significant contribution to our ability to understand cyclical movements in general business.

Wesley Clair Mitchell suggested a number of years ago the importance of efforts to isolate what he called "characteristic cyclical timing" when he wrote:

> It is not surprising to find that the bulk of . . . time series fluctuate in unison. Nor is it surprising to find that many . . . series lead or lag at business-cycle troughs and peaks. . . . Indeed, these differences of characteristic timing make it easier to grasp the way in which business cycles propagate (I do not say cause) themselves. But that is a later part of the complicated story.[2]

The story is no less complicated today. But the importance of movements in consumer credit is assuredly greater today because of the growth in consumer credit.

[2] Wesley Clair Mitchell, *What Happens During Business Cycles: A Progress Report,* New York, National Bureau of Economic Research, 1951 pp. 78–79.

2

Total Consumer Credit

CLASSIFICATION AND DEFINITION OF COMPONENTS

AT THIS POINT we will indicate briefly what is included in the major components of consumer credit.[1] The term "consumer credit" as currently used by the Federal Reserve ". . . includes short- and intermediate-term credit that is extended through regular business channels to finance the purchase of commodities and services for personal consumption, or to refinance debts incurred for such purposes."[2] As noted earlier, consumer credit may be broadly divided into instalment and noninstalment credit. The latter measures the ". . . obligations of consumers scheduled to be repaid in a single payment."[3] It includes single payment loans held principally by commercial banks; charge accounts held by department stores, mail-order houses, and other retail outlets (e.g., furniture stores), and general credit-card business; and service credit, which includes credit for medical care, public utilities, education and recreation, funeral and legal expenses, etc. Many kinds of noninstalment credit have become important relatively recently.

Instalment credit includes all consumer credit scheduled to be repaid in two or more separate payments. There are four types: automobile paper, by far the largest single sector; loans for other consumer goods; home repair and modernization loans; and personal loans.

[1] For a full description of consumer credit and its components as usually defined, see *Supplement to Banking and Monetary Statistics*, Section 16, (New) Consumer Credit, Federal Reserve System, September 1965.

[2] *Ibid.*, p. 2.

[3] *Ibid.*, p. 24.

GROWTH OF CONSUMER CREDIT

We shall begin by observing the over-all growth and cyclical sensitivity of consumer credit and its component parts. As is apparent in Chart 1, consumer credit growth has been concentrated largely in three periods. The use of credit for consumer durables was first intoduced on a large scale in the twenties, with a peak in 1929. The second period corresponded to the period of recovery from the Great Depression and reached a peak in 1941 at the onset of U.S. participation in World War II. Both of these periods of growth were small, however, compared with the third, which began at the end of World War II and has continued ever since. Consumer credit outstanding has more than quadrupled since 1950, increasing from about $20 billion to almost $100 billion. The absolute growth during this third period as well as the growth relative to the earlier ones has been very substantial. Instalment credit (including automobile credit) and noninstalment credit have both shared in this growth, generally conforming to the pattern just discussed. Noninstalment credit differed to the extent that it showed only modest expansion during the second period.

While the over-all trends are thus similar, some changes in relative importance are worth noting. In the prewar period the importance of instalment relative to noninstalment paper in total consumer credit tended to shift back and forth. Since World War II instalment credit has been consistently larger, and has grown consistently faster, than noninstalment credit; automobile paper alone, since the early 1950's, has exceeded total noninstalment credit in absolute size. In the past few years the gap between instalment and noninstalment credit has appeared to be narrowing somewhat, probably as a result of the rapid growth in credit forms like revolving charge accounts, etc.

Chart 1 makes it clear that the credit industry is quite sensitive cyclically. Noninstalment credit has been the least unstable in this regard.[4] Indeed, its only cyclical manifestation in the postwar period has been decelerated growth in a few recessions. Automobile credit, on the other hand, seems to be the most volatile, having reacted to every business cycle during the period covered except the postwar readjustment cycle and the 1948–49 recession. Even in these two cycles none of the series declined. These relationships will be explored in detail subsequently.

[4] The growth of service credit as well as the increased importance of credit cards may render this sector more sensitive to the cycle in the future. The evidence is still incomplete.

CHART 1

Consumer Credit and Its Major Components, 1919–67

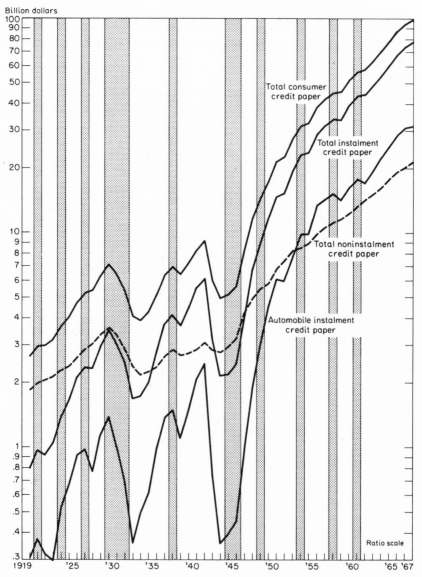

NOTE: Shaded areas represent business cycle contractions; white areas, expansions.

SOURCE: *1919–62*—Supplement to *Banking and Monetary Statistics,* Section 16, p. 33; *1963–67—Federal Reserve Bulletin,* February 1968, p. A. 48.

Consumer Credit and GNP

It is well known that in series with rising trends, yearly variations are likely to become larger in absolute terms. Consumer credit, its instalment credit component, and gross national product have all grown greatly in the United States during the period under review. In investi-

CHART 2

Total Consumer Credit, Total Instalment Credit, and GNP, as a Percentage of the Previous Year, 1919–67

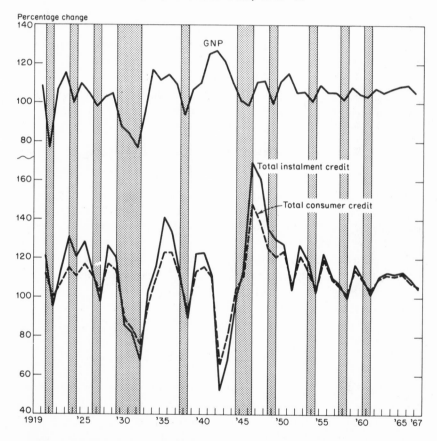

NOTE: Shaded areas represent business cycle contractions; white areas, expansions.

SOURCE: *GNP—1919–67—Survey of Current Business; Consumer Credit— 1919–62—Supplement to Banking and Monetary Statistics; 1963–67—Federal Reserve Bulletin,* February 1968.

gating the cyclical impact of the credit series, it is therefore helpful to consider their variability *relative* to the variability in gross national product. Can one say that the per cent variation over the cycle has changed for either of the two credit series compared with the per cent variation that has occurred in GNP?

It seems clear from Chart 2 that apart from the Great Depression and the early forties, the relative variability over the cycle in the credit series has not changed greatly (it is, for example, approximately the same in the prewar and postwar periods). But it is important to note, too, that in general most of the rises in both measures of credit represented larger percentage increases than did the rises in GNP at roughly corresponding periods. (The two credit series usually reach peaks at the same time; the peaks in GNP are not always coincident, but are usually close.) Moreover, these greater percentage increases in the credit series than in GNP during expansions are not matched by larger decreases in credit relative to GNP during contractions, when all three series usually have decreased by comparable percentages.

TIMING OF CONSUMER CREDIT DURING BUSINESS CYCLES

An analysis of the timing patterns of consumer credit outstanding suggests why the bulk of our attention must be focused on the instalment credit component. Chart 3 and Table 1 indicate the relevant information. Chart 4 summarizes the results. Clearly it would be preferable to have more data so that our analysis could include more than one postwar and two prewar cycles. While generalizations or "averages" based on such a small sample must be viewed with caution, it is well to remember that we are able to examine the record of the recent past during a period of almost 40 years. This is quite long by the standards of much current analysis, and covers the bulk of the period during which consumer credit was reasonably well established in the U.S. economy.

In Chart 3, total consumer credit outstanding clearly has been sensitive to changes in aggregate economic activity at least as far back as 1929. But the sensitivity has been less pronounced since World War II. In the case of noninstalment credit, some cyclical sensitivity evident in the prewar period has entirely disappeared since the war, except for a slight decrease in the rate of increase during recessions. Chart 3 also suggests that, where comparisons can be made, total consumer

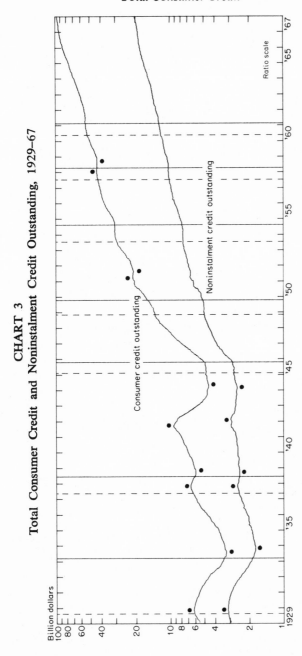

CHART 3

Total Consumer Credit and Noninstalment Credit Outstanding, 1929–67

NOTE: Vertical broken lines represent business cycle peaks; vertical solid lines, troughs. Dots identify peaks and troughs of specific cycles.

SOURCE: Board of Governors, Federal Reserve System.

credit outstanding and its noninstalment credit component lag behind the business cycle generally. Table 1 indicates the nature of these lags in greater detail.

Table 1 shows that total consumer credit outstanding has lagged behind every business cycle for which comparison is possible, perhaps reflecting the increasing cyclical insensitivity of its noninstalment credit component. Although consumer credit outstanding has reacted to general cyclical movements mainly by tending to flatten out rather than decline during the postwar period, the timing relationships appear to be about the same as before World War II. Compared to business cycles, the lags appear to be consistently longer at cyclical peaks than at troughs.

Table 1 suggests that instalment credit has exhibited average timing at peaks and troughs similar to that for total consumer credit outstanding. Noninstalment credit shows the same lag pattern as total consumer credit outstanding, but cyclical sensitivity has disappeared in the postwar period. Instalment credit has continued to be cyclically sensitive in this period. The table thus indicates that the instalment credit component has been responsible for any cyclical sensitivity in total consumer credit in the years after World War II. The relative cyclical stability of noninstalment credit should not go unnoticed, however, because this sector has, as indicated above, been growing at a relatively rapid rate during recent years.

The timing comparisons themselves are enumerated in Table 2 together with analytical information on the measures of average timing that were just considered. The patterns of instability revealed by the major components of consumer credit are summarized in Chart 4, which indicates in schematic fashion the turning points in total consumer credit outstanding, instalment credit outstanding, automobile credit outstanding, and noninstalment credit outstanding. It is clearly seen that all measures of outstanding credit exhibited greater conformity to the business cycle during the prewar period. They diverged from the business cycle pattern during the war, but moved together presenting an extra cycle in 1938–44. This reflected production restrictions, accompanied by the imposition of Regulation W, and the resulting virtual elimination of new instalment credit during this period.

The chart underscores the postwar divergence of instalment credit, which continues to show cyclical sensitivity, from noninstalment credit. The pattern of conformity of instalment credit to the business cycle established during the prewar period is less complete in the postwar

Table 1

Timing Analysis, Total Consumer, Noninstalment, and Instalment Credit Outstanding at Business Cycle Peaks and Troughs, 1929–67

	Peaks							Troughs					
Bus. Cycle Peak	Total Consumer Credit Outstanding	Lead (−) or Lag (+)	Total Noninstal. Credit Outstanding	Lead (−) or Lag (+)	Total Instal. Credit Outstanding	Lead (−) or Lag (+)	Bus. Cycle Trough	Total Consumer Credit Outstanding	Lead (−) or Lag (+)	Total Noninstal. Credit Outstanding	Lead (−) or Lag (+)	Total Instal. Credit Outstanding	Lead (−) or Lag (+)
	(1)	(2)	(3)	(4)	(5)	(6)		(7)	(8)	(9)	(10)	(11)	(12)
8/29	10/29	+2½	10/29	+2½	10/29	+2½	3/33	7/33	+4½	11/33	+8½	5/33	+2½
5/37	10/37	+5½	11/37	+6½	9/37	+4½	6/38	8/38	+2½	10/38	+4½	10/38	+4½
2/45	8/41	—	1/42	—	8/41	—	10/45	NT		2/44	—	4/44	—
11/48	NT		NT		NT		10/49	NT		NT		NT	
7/53	NT		NT		3/51	—	8/54	NT		NT		7/51	—
7/57	3/51	—	NT		2/54	+7½	4/58	7/51	—	NT		6/54	−1½
5/60	NT		NT		1/58	+6½	2/61	6/58	+2½	NT		9/58	+5½
					12/60	+7½		NT				4/61	+2½
Prewar Period (1929–38)													
Average		+4.0		+4.5		+3.5			+3.5		+6.5		+3.5
Average deviation		+1.5		+2.0		+1.0			+1.0		+2.0		+1.0
Postwar Period (1945–67)													
Average						+7.2							+2.2
Average deviation						+0.4							+2.4
Whole Period (1929–67)													
Average		+4.8		+4.5		+5.7			+3.2		+6.5		+2.7
Average deviation		+1.6		+2.0		+1.8			+0.9		+2.0		+1.8

NT = No turn.
NOTE: Figured at end of month. Leads and lags in months.
SOURCE: *Federal Reserve Bulletin.*

CHART 4

Specific Cycles in Consumer Credit Outstanding at Business Cycle Peaks
and Troughs, 1929–67

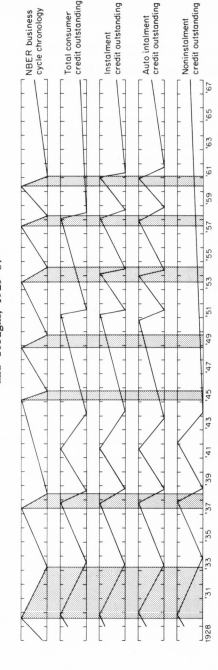

NOTE: Shaded areas represent business cycle contractions; white areas, expansions.
SOURCE: *Federal Reserve Bullein,* selected issues.

Table 2

Summary of Timing: Consumer, Instalment, and Noninstalment Credit at Business Cycles, 1929–67

Line	Consumer Credit Outstanding	Noninstalment Credit	Instalment Credit Outstanding
1. Number of business cycle turns covered	14	14	14
2. Number of leads	0	0	1
3. Number of rough coincidences[a]	3 (0)	1 (0)	4 (0)
4. Number of lags	6	4	9
5. Number of timing comparisons	6	4	10
6. Number of business cycle turns skipped	8	10	4
7. Number of extra specific cycle turns	4	2	4
8. Median lead (−) or lag (+) at peak	+5½	+4½	+6½
9. Median lead (−) or lag (+) at trough	+2½	+6½	+2½
10. Mean lead (−) or lag (+) at peak	+4.8	+4.5	+5.7
11. Mean lead (−) or lag (+) at trough	+3.2	+6.5	+2.7
12. Average deviation at peak[b]	1.6	2.0	1.8
13. Average deviation at trough[b]	0.9	2.0	1.8

[a]Rough coincidences include exact coincidences (shown in parentheses) and leads or lags of three months or less. The total number of timing comparisons (line 5) is equal to the total number of leads, exact coincidences, and lags.

[b]Average deviations have been computed about the mean leads and lags reported in lines 10 and 11.

NOTE: Computed at the end of the month.

SOURCE: Federal Reserve Board.

period; instalment credit and its automobile component presented an extra cycle in connection with the Korean War; moreover, instalment credit skipped the mild recession immediately after World War II.

We may conclude, therefore, that the instalment credit component of consumer credit has exhibited the greatest cyclical volatility since 1945.

3

Instalment Credit

RELATION TO DISPOSABLE PERSONAL INCOME

WE HAVE SEEN that instalment credit is the part of consumer credit most sensitive to business cycles. Now we want to know how important it is in the economy and if its importance has changed over time.

Chart 5 shows instalment credit extensions, repayments, and outstandings as percentages of disposable personal income for 1929–67. From this, we can determine the relative impact of business cycles on income and on credit, as well as the relative rates of growth of credit and income. Thus, if credit were growing at precisely the same rate as disposable income there would be no upward movement in the chart; or if the rates of change of the credit series exactly matched the cyclical rates of change in income the credit series would represent the same percentage of income during expansion and contraction and cycles would not be visible in the chart. In Chart 5, clearly both the secular and the cyclical relationships of instalment credit to disposable income show changes of importance.

The major finding is the striking increase in credit relative to disposable personal income since the end of World War II. Extensions have reached as high as 16 per cent of disposable personal income, although 13–14 per cent is more usual for the most recent period. This compares with percentages not much higher than 10 per cent for the prewar period. Outstandings and repayments have also reached higher levels relative to disposable personal income in the postwar period. Thus, despite the great growth in disposable personal income over the years since 1929, instalment credit, however measured, has grown at an even faster rate.

Once again, the cyclical volatility of credit can be observed in Chart

CHART 5

Instalment Credit Extensions, Repayments, and Outstandings as a
Percentage of Disposable Personal Income, 1929–67

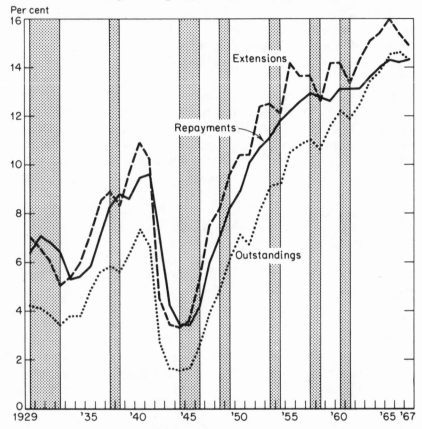

NOTE: Shaded areas represent business cycle contractions; white areas, expansions.

SOURCE: *Federal Reserve Bulletins* and OBE, *Business Statistics.*

5. In every recession shown there, with the exception of the first two postwar recessions, all three measures of instalment credit decreased relative to disposable personal income.[1]

We may note, too, the precipitous decline in the relative importance of credit during World War II. Production restrictions sharply affected both automobile buying and credit extensions. The bulk were affected

[1] Repayments did not fall in the first three postwar recessions.

by Regulation W. The consequence for the instalment credit purchase of cars is clearly shown in Chart 5.[2]

Table 3, closely related to Chart 5, indicates (in millions of dollars) the total change during expansions and contractions in both disposable personal income and total instalment credit outstanding during all the cyclical episodes since 1929.[3] These changes have also been shown on a per quarter basis so that it is possible to compare the average quarterly change in the amplitude of the changes in both income and instalment credit outstanding during the cycle phases of varying lengths. The greater severity of the prewar recessions shows up in quantifiable fashion. The total (net) change in both disposable income and in instalment credit outstanding was negative (the only case in the total comparisons at the bottom of the table for which this was true), but the percentage ratio is also the smallest, indicating the relatively insignificant size of instalment credit relative to disposable income as well as their relative volatilities, at that time. For all the other comparisons the percentage ratios are positive because the (net) totals during the postwar expansions and contractions are positive.[4] The percentage ratios are much higher during both expansions and contractions in the postwar period and we thus have an indication of the increase in the magnitude of the impact which swings in credit have exhibited relative to the swings in disposable income. Furthermore, the comparisons suggest that the swings in credit relative to income have been far greater during expansions than they have during contractions. For the entire period, the change in instalment credit outstanding appears to have constituted about one-fifth of the change in disposable income during both expansions and contractions, although the variability, as indicated in the specific ratios, is very great indeed.

[2] Because we shall subsequently be concerned with the automobile component of instalment credit, it is appropriate to point out that the pattern indicated in Chart 5 for total instalment credit corresponds in most important particulars to the pattern for automobile credit alone. Auto credit extensions have reached as much as 6 per cent of total disposable income in the postwar period, though they were usually no more than about 3 per cent in the prewar period. Outstandings and repayments behaved in the same fashion indicated in Chart 5 for total instalment credit.

[3] The only exception is for the termination of the series arbitrarily at the end of 1969, which was not an official turning point in the NBER business cycle chronology.

[4] The few times in which either disposable income or instalment credit declined absolutely during contractions are more than offset by the times when they increased, albeit customarily at decreasing rates, during contraction.

Table 3
Relation Between Change in Disposable Personal Income and
Net Change in Instalment Credit Outstanding: Cyclical Expansions
and Contractions During Calendar Years, 1929–69

Calendar year (1)	Cycle Phase C–Contraction E–Expansion (2)	Change in Disposable Personal Income		Change in Instalment Credit Outstanding		Percentage Ratio[a] (col. 6 ÷ col. 4 × 100) (7)	Change in Percentage (8)
		Total (3)	Per Quarter (4)	Total (5)	Per Quarter (6)		
1929–32	C	− 34,567	−2,881	− 1,852	− 154	+ 5.35	—
1932–37	E	+ 22,502	+1,125	+ 2,446	+ 122	+ 10.84	+ 5.49
1937–38	C	− 5,713	−1,428	− 432	− 108	+ 7.56	− 3.28
1938–41[b]	E	+ 27,195	+2,266	+ 2,399	+ 200	+ 8.83	+ 1.27
1944–46[b]	C	—	—	—	—	—	—
1946–48	E	+ 29,117	+640	+ 4,824	+ 603	+ 16.57	—
1948–49	C	+ 553	− 138	+ 2,594	+ 648	−469.57	−486.14
1949–53	E	+ 63,979	+3,999	+ 11,415	+ 713	+ 17.83	+487.40
1953–54	C	+ 4,881	+1,220	+ 563	+ 141	+ 11.56	+ 6.27
1954–57	E	+ 51,079	+4,257	+ 10,299	+ 858	+ 20.16	+ 8.60
1957–58	C	+ 10,302	+2,576	− 255	− 64	− 2.48	− 22.64
1958–60	E	+ 31,218	+3,902	+ 9,190	+1,149	+ 29.45	+ 31.93
1960–61	C	+ 14,380	+3,595	+ 695	+ 174	+ 4.84	− 24.61
1961–69[c]	E	+265,200	+8,288	+ 64,200	+2,006	+ 24.20	+ 19.36
Totals Prewar (1929–41)	C	− 40,280		− 2,284		+ 5.67	
	E	+ 49,697		+ 4,845		+ 9.75	

(continued)

Table 3 (concluded)

Calendar Year (1)	Cycle Phase C–Contraction E–Expansion. (2)	Change in Disposable Personal Income		Change in Instalment Credit Outstanding		Percentage Ratio[a] – (col. 6 ÷ col. 4 × 100) (7)	Change in Percentage (8)
		Total (3)	Per Quarter (4)	Total (5)	Per Quarter (6)		
Postwar (1946–69)	C	+ 29,010		+ 3,597		+ 12.40	
	E	+440,593		+ 99,928		+ 22.68	
Both (1929–41, 1946–69)	C	– 11,270		+ 1,313		– 11.65	
	E	+490,290		+104,773		+ 21.37	

[a]A + sign indicates increases in both credit and income in the same direction; a – sign denotes change in the offsetting direction. Calculations are based on per quarter comparisons and differ from totals only due to rounding errors.

[b]The 1938–44 expansion has been truncated to 1938–41, since after 1941 the consumption and instalment credit sectors were powerfully affected by wartime controls. The 1944–46 contraction has been eliminated for the same reasons.

[c]The end of 1969 has been utilized in the calculations, but was, of course, not an official NBER turning point.

NOTE: Disposable personal income and net change in instalment credit are in millions of dollars.

SOURCE: Disposable personal income—*The National Income and Product Accounts of the U.S., 1929–1965 Statistical Tables*, Department of Commerce, O.B.E., pp. 32–33; Instalment credit–Federal Reserve Bank, *Supplement to Banking and Monetary Statistics*, p. 95, and *Federal Reserve Bulletin*, selected issues.

The most significant finding of the table, however, is the increased importance since World War II of instalment credit relative to disposable personal income during business cycles. The variability in the percentage ratios (column 8) has grown as well, relative to the prewar period, and here the signs still conform usually to the stage of the cycle, indicating that only rarely has either credit change or income change remained immune to the impact of cyclical forces.

CONFORMITY TO BUSINESS CYCLES

We have thus far examined only the total amount of credit outstanding. Three other basic measures of instalment credit activity are extensions of new credit, repayments of existing credit, and net change in outstandings. The four basic credit measures—outstandings, extensions, repayments, and net change—are related definitionally: Net change is the difference in outstandings between two successive dates like months or quarters, and net change is also equal to the algebraic sum of extensions $(+)$ and repayments $(-)$. The data on these four basic measures over the 1929–67 period constitute the basic record, and are presented in Appendix Tables C1-C4. It is turns in these measures that we will now analyze.[5]

We begin by considering the degree to which all these measures of instalment credit exhibit basic conformity to the cyclical record of aggregate economic activity in the United States. Specifically, does instalment credit as measured by extensions, repayments, outstandings, and net credit change in outstandings exhibit cycles that conform generally to American business cycles between 1929 and 1967? Conformity must be established and evaluated before the pattern of turns, which we consider subsequently, can be properly evaluated. If there are many skipped cycles or many extra cycles, for example, the results of an analysis of timing would have little significance. Charts 6 and 7 show the movement in these four measures of instalment credit during this period.

The general cyclical conformity of net credit change, extensions, and outstandings for both total instalment credit and total automobile

[5] In unadjusted data, outstandings at the beginning of month t plus extensions during t minus repayments during t must equal outstandings at the end of t; thus net change in outstandings between the beginning and end of t will necessarily equal extensions minus repayments during t. However, in seasonally adjusted data, since outstandings, extensions, and repayments are separately adjusted, it will not generally be true that seasonally adjusted extensions minus seasonally adjusted repayments will equal seasonally adjusted change in outstandings.

CHART 6

Instalment Credit Extended, Repaid, and Outstanding, 1929–67

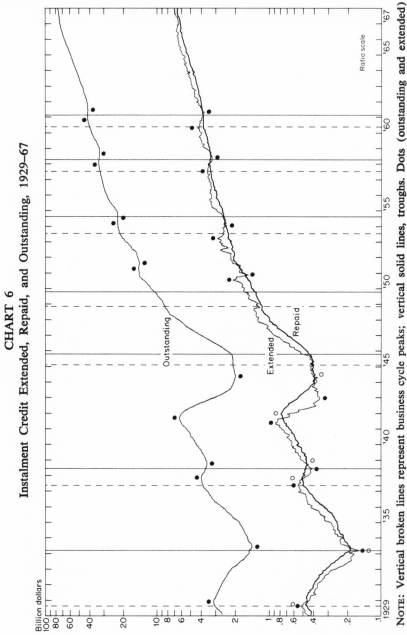

NOTE: Vertical broken lines represent business cycle peaks; vertical solid lines, troughs. Dots (outstanding and extended) or circles (repaid) identify peaks and troughs of specific cycles.

SOURCE: Board of Governors, Federal Reserve System.

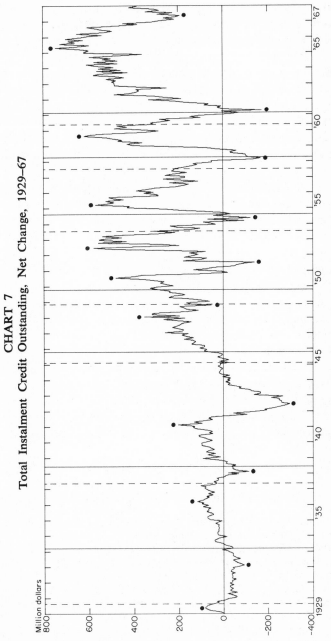

CHART 7

Total Instalment Credit Outstanding, Net Change, 1929–67

NOTE: Vertical broken lines represent business cycle peaks; vertical solid lines, troughs. Dots identify peaks and troughs of specific cycles.

SOURCE: Board of Governors, Federal Reserve System.

credit throughout the period under review is shown clearly in Chart 8. The conformity of these measures is somewhat greater during the prewar period. Although the repayments series for both auto and total instalment credit also conform during the prewar period, they fail to conform in the postwar period. Indeed, the repayments series have shown no cycles at all in the period since 1945. All the credit series show a wartime cycle in the early 1940's (previously considered in connection with credit outstanding), which does not coincide with the reference chronology. This cycle is associated principally with the wartime production restriction but was also affected by the imposition of Regulation W.[6]

All the credit series skip the postwar readjustment cycle (1945) except auto credit extensions. Actually we shall see that this is a mild recession in extensions, and that outstandings and repayments reflect this episode, too, although not sufficiently strongly to produce turning points.

The pattern of conformity during the 1948–49 recession is interesting. The postwar demand for consumer durables was so strong and the use of credit as a means of paying for these durables was growing so rapidly that only the most volatile of the credit series, net credit change, reflects this recession. The implications of this will be considered in the subsequent consideration of the timing pattern.

We find that all the credit series (again with the exception of the two repayments series) show an extra cycle in 1950–51, which can be related to the Korean War and the reimposition of Regulation W. All the credit series except the repayments series exhibit conformity to the 1953–54 cyclical pattern, though the timing here will be of considerable interest to us.

The series dealing with automobile net change in outstandings and with extensions show an extra cycle in 1955–56, which was associated with the liberalization in instalment credit terms for autos in 1955.[7]

[6] For a full discussion of Regulation W, see Robert Paul Shay, *Regulation W: Experiment in Credit Control,* Orono, Maine, 1953.

[7] Considerable attention, both within the automobile industry and among economists, has been paid to the experience of 1955–56. The rapid liberalization of terms in 1955 may well have encouraged many who might otherwise not have purchased an automobile until 1956 to purchase in the earlier year. This produced a greater increase in sales in 1955, but because terms could not (or at any rate did not) continue easing at the same rate in 1956 as in 1954–55, sales in 1956 decreased. By luring some of the 1956 customers into the market in 1955, the easing of terms in 1955 may well have contributed to this extra cycle.

CHART 8

Chronology of Specific Cycles in Four Measures of Instalment Credit and Four Measures of Auto Credit at Business Cycle Peaks and Troughs, 1929–67

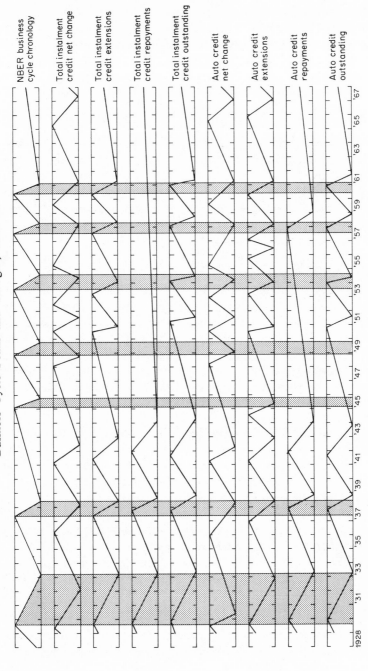

NBER business cycle chronology

Total instalment credit net change

Total instalment credit extensions

Total instalment credit repayments

Total instalment credit outstanding

Auto credit net change

Auto credit extensions

Auto credit repayments

Auto credit outstanding

NOTE: Shaded areas represent business cycle contractions; white areas, expansions.
SOURCE: See Charts 6, 7, 10, and 13.

After 1956 all the credit series conform reasonably well to the third and fourth postwar recessions, although it must be emphasized that by "conformity" we here mean little more than a cyclical movement in the credit series that can be associated with a corresponding movement in the business cycles.

It is possible to argue that the conformity of these series to the business cycle depends more on whether the cycles involved are severe or mild and that there have not been significant changes in their relationships to business cycles since World War II. Unfortunately it is impossible to test this properly. The two prewar recessions were the most severe of any included. Data are not available to examine the degree of conformity exhibited by credit movements during cycles in the 1920's; moreover, instalment credit was in its infancy during this earlier period. Despite some variation in the intensity or severity of the postwar cycles, all have been relatively mild. One of the more severe recessions occurred in 1948–49 and the conformity of instalment credit series during this period was, for the reasons already discussed, poor. Other than that (and the immediate postwar cycle) one could not rank the degree of conformity in each recession period with any degree of precision. Nonetheless, it is clear that the series dealing with instalment credit reveal a rather high degree of conformity to the cycles in aggregate economic activity throughout the period under review. We may therefore conclude that it is appropriate to examine the pattern of turns in these series more closely.

TIMING DURING BUSINESS CYCLES

A detailed listing of the turning points in each of the four measures of instalment credit and the timing relationships of each turn to the business cycle turn are given in Tables 1, 4, and 5. In Table 6, for peaks and for troughs, we have indicated the average timing relationship for the prewar period, the postwar period, and for the entire period, including in each average all the comparable turns.[8]

In Table 6, it is clear that for each cycle except 1929–33 and 1948–49 the average lead in net change in outstandings is much longer at peaks than at troughs. The disparity has been greater, but only slightly so, since the war. There has been variability in the lead, more

[8] That is, specific turns have been related wherever possible to reference turns. In effect, only the skipped cycles and extra cycles were not considered.

Table 4

Timing Analysis, Total Instalment Credit Outstanding,
Extensions, and Repayments at Business Cycle Peaks and Troughs, 1929–67

	Peaks						Troughs					
Bus. Cycle Peak	Net Change in Total Instal. Credit (1)	Lead (–) or Lag (+) (2)	Total Instal. Credit Extensions (3)	Lead (–) or Lag (+) (4)	Total Instal. Credit Repayments (5)	Lead (–) or Lag (+) (6)	Bus. Cycle Trough (7)	Net Change in Total Instal. Credit	Lead (–) or Lag (+) (8)	Total Instal. Credit Extensions (9)	Lead (–) or Lag (+) (10)	Total Instal. Credit Repayments (11)	Lead (–) or Lag (+) (12)
8/29	5/29	– 3	8/29	0	9/29	+1	3/33	2/32	–13	3/33	0	3/33	0
5/37	3/36	–14	5/37	0	10/37	+5	6/38	2/38	– 4	6/38	0	8/38	+2
2/41	2/41	–	5/41	–	12/41	–	6/42	6/42	–	12/42	–	2/44	–
2/45	NT		NT	–	NT	–	10/45	NT	–	NT	–	NT	–
11/48	1/48	–10	NT	–	NT	–	10/49	10/48	–12	NT	–	NT	–
	7/50	–	7/50	–				7/51	–	11/50	–	NT	–
7/53	6/52	–13	3/53	–4	NT	–	8/54	5/54	– 3	1/54	–7	NT	–
7/57	3/55	–28	7/57	0	NT	–	4/58	3/58	– 1	5/58	–1	NT	–
5/60	8/59	– 9	4/60	–1	NT	–	2/61	4/61	+ 2	4/61	+2	NT	–
	4/65	–						5/67	–				

NT = No turn.

NOTE: Leads and lags are in months.

SOURCE: *Federal Reserve Bulletin.*

Table 5

Summary of Timing of Instalment Credit: Net Credit Change,
Extensions, and Repayments at Business Cycles, 1929–67

Line	Net Credit Change	Extensions	Repayments
1. Number of business cycle turns covered	14	14	14
2. Number of leads	11	3	0
3. Number of rough coincidences[a]	4(0)	8(5)	3(1)
4. Number of lags	1	2	3
5. Number of timing comparisons	12	10	4
6. Number of business cycle turns skipped	2	4	10
7. Number of extra specific cycle turns	6	4	2
8. Median lead (−) or lag (+) at peak	−11½	0	+3
9. Median lead (−) or lag (+) at trough	−3½	0	+1
10. Mean lead (−) or lag (+) at peak	−12.8	−1.0	+3.0
11. Mean lead (−) or lag (+) at trough	−5.2	−0.8	+1.0
12. Average deviation at peak[b]	5.5	1.2	2.0
13. Average deviation at trough[b]	4.9	2.5	1.0

[a]Rough coincidences include exact coincidences (shown in parentheses) and leads or lags of three months or less. The total number of timing comparisons (line 5) is equal to the total number of leads, exact coincidences, and lags.

[b]Average deviations have been computed from the mean leads and lags reported in lines 10 and 11.

NOTE: Computed at the end of the month.

SOURCE: Federal Reserve Board.

at peaks than at troughs, but the pattern is quite clear. Net change in credit outstanding is extremely volatile, reflecting, in effect, the difference between extensions and repayments.

Extensions in instalment credit present no significant divergence from the business cycle turns in Table 4. At both peaks and troughs there has been a slight average lead in the postwar period, but this is due entirely to the 1953–54 experience. This consistency shows up in comparatively small average deviations for the period as a whole.

Repayments need little further comment. They lagged during three of four turns prior to the war and have not exhibited downturns since then (Table 4). Credit has grown so rapidly that all postwar recessions have either not been reflected at all in the repayments series or have taken the form of a decreased rate of increase. In this connection it is important to remember that because of the increased importance of

Table 6

Average Timing and Deviation for Four Measures of Total Instalment
Credit at Business Cycle Peaks and Troughs, 1929–67
(in months)

	Peaks			Troughs		
	Prewar	Postwar	Entire Period	Prewar	Postwar	Entire Period
Net credit change						
Average	−8.5(2)	−15.04(4)	−12.8(6)	−8.5(2)	−3.5(4)	−5.2(6)
Average deviation	5.5	6.5	5.5	5.5	4.2	4.9
Extensions[a]						
Average	0 (2)	− 1.7(3)	− 1.0(5)	0 (2)	−1.3(3)	−0.8(5)
Average deviation	0	1.6	1.2	0	3.8	2.5
Outstandings[b]						
Average	+3.5(2)	+ 7.2(3)	+ 5.7(5)	+3.5(2)	+2.2(3)	+2.7(5)
Average deviation	1.0	0.4	1.8	1.0	2.4	1.8
Repayments[c]						
Average	+3.0(2)	NT	+ 3.0(2)	+1.0(2)	NT	+1.0(2)
Average deviation	2.0		3.0	1.0		1.0

[a]Extensions skip one postwar peak and one trough.
[b]Outstandings skip one postwar peak and one trough.
[c]All prewar turns.
NT = No turns.
NOTE: Numbers in parentheses show the number of reference cycle comparisons included in each average. All instalment credit series skip the 1945 business cycle contraction. Prewar averages for all series cover the same reference cycle turns and are comparable. Postwar averages do not refer to the same turns and are not comparable. For details, see Tables 1 and 4.
SOURCE: Tables 1 and 4.

automatic stabilizers the postwar period is characterized by an increased ability of personal income (and more importantly, disposable personal income) to hold up during recessions.[9] We have

[9] The immediate reason for the cyclical insensitivity of repayments since World War II is that scheduled repayments are spread out over time so that they behave, in effect, like a moving average of extensions. They must, therefore, have a smaller amplitude than extensions: if the cycles in the latter are small or short enough, they will disappear altogether in repayments. We have considered this possibility in some detail below in connection with the discussion of automobile credit.

already noted that credit has grown more rapidly than income, but the relative stability of income has undoubtedly led to the disappearance of cycles in repayments.

Total credit outstanding, like its net change, presents a clear pattern of divergence from the business cycle—this time in the form of a lag. Credit outstanding is, of course, a stock, whereas net change in credit outstanding, which we saw in Table 4 typically leads the reference dates, is a flow. It is not uncommon for stocks to turn after flows (e.g., inventories). Table 1, already considered, shows that instalment credit outstanding has lagged at all five of the peaks since 1929 for which timing comparisons can be made. There has been small variability around the average lag of about five months. The lag has been smaller (something over two months) but equally variable at troughs. At both peaks and troughs there has been no clear-cut indication of a change in the pattern from the prewar to the postwar period.

Our basic data concerning the timing of net credit change, extension, and repayment of instalment credit are summarized in Table 5. The implications of this pattern of turns in instalment credit can best be considered if we look as well at the relationships of these averages to each other. This is done in Table 6 and suggests that these turns are not only related to the reference chronology in a fairly systematic way, but also to each other.

The general pattern in the turning points summarized in Table 6 is quite clear both at the peaks and to a lesser extent at the troughs. Net credit change turns first—leading by ten to twelve months at the peak and by about five months at the trough. Extensions tend to turn in a manner roughly coincident with the business cycle turns and show smaller variability at turning points than net credit change.[10] Repayments and outstandings typically lag. Repayments, however, have turned so seldom that the evidence for a lag is slight. There is no question, of course, that repayments must, by their very nature, lag behind extensions. This pattern of turns—net credit change first, followed by extensions, and finally by repayments and outstandings—is almost completely consistent throughout the period under review.

Before attempting to explain the pattern of turns shown in Table 6 it is appropriate to ask how consistently this *average* pattern is found in the *individual* cycles. Except for repayments, the pattern of turns is present at all five peaks that can be associated with the business

---

[10] Compare the average deviations in Table 6.

cycle peaks between 1929 and 1967. The relatively high average lead for net credit change, as well as the high variability, it should be noted, is heavily influenced by the long lead in 1957, which in turn was the result of the extremely rapid growth in credit in 1955 resulting from the easing of credit terms and the other circumstances discussed earlier. At troughs the order of turns is a bit less consistent. There are several that are coincident and several ties. Of the five comparable troughs, the sequence of turns is clearly broken twice (1953 and 1960), and is clearly visible three times (1929, 1937, and 1957).[11]

The economic implications of this pattern can best be considered in conjunction with Chart 9, which is an effort to explain why the lead in the turning points in the net credit change series is so much longer at business cycle peaks than at troughs. Because net credit change measures the change in outstandings, which in turn is the excess of extensions over repayments, the explanation ultimately involves all four of the measures of credit.[12]

a. *Cycle effect.* Part A of Chart 9 portrays the effect of the interrelationship of extensions and repayments on the timing of turns in net credit change. Specifically, it shows that, when a lagging series (repayments) is subtracted from a coincident series (extensions), the difference (net credit change) leads both series at peaks and troughs.[13]

b. *Trend effect.* One reason for the pattern of turns in net credit change, however, is that throughout the postwar period repayments

---

[11] The timing relationships indicated reflect, of course, the underlying process by which credit outstanding changes over time. The fundamental pattern was well described by Gottfried Haberler for the pre-World War II period (see Gottfried Haberler, *Consumer Instalment Credit and Economic Fluctuations,* NBER, New York, 1942).

More recently the timing relationships have been examined in Paul W. Mc-Cracken, James C. T. Mao, and Cedric Fricke, *Consumer Instalment Credit and Public Policy,* Michigan Business Studies, Vol. XVII, No. 1, 1965. This study examines only quarterly data, and while it finds a general pattern of conformity to the business cycle, the timing relationships, as would be expected, are less sharply defined than in the monthly data.

[12] If C_{t-1} and C_t represent credit outstanding at the end of periods $t-1$ and t, respectively, E_t is extensions during time t, and R_t repayments during the same period, then $C_{t-1} + E_t - R_t = C_t$ and $\Delta C_t = E_t - R_t$.

[13] We may add that, though the repayments evidence is very limited, as noted, for all four of the important reference turns preceding World War II, extensions turned before repayments (though in one case the lead was only one month). The turns utilized as the reference chronology in Chart 9 refer to extensions, not the business cycle turns.

CHART 9

The Pattern of Turns in Net Credit Change, a Schematic Explanation

Part. A. Cycle Effect

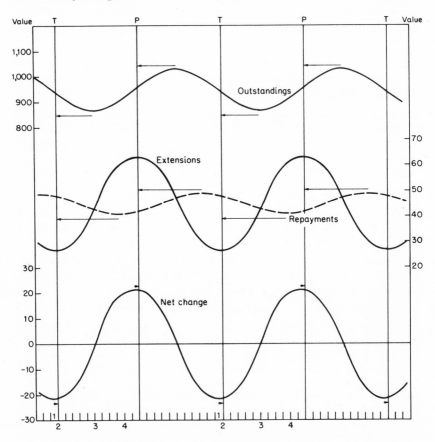

have reflected cyclical changes only through increasing at decreasing rates during recessions, whereas extensions have continued to fluctuate cyclically. The result of this rising trend in repayments is to make net credit change reflect the movement of extensions but with a less rapidly rising trend (Part B of Chart 9). The rising trend of repayments is subtracted from extensions to obtain the net credit change, and the effect is to make the peaks in net credit change occur earlier than in extensions, and the troughs later.

Thus, there are two influences (a cyclical effect and a trend effect) making peaks in net credit change lead extensions and business cycle peaks, whereas at troughs one influence (the cycle effect) tends to

Part B. Trend Effect

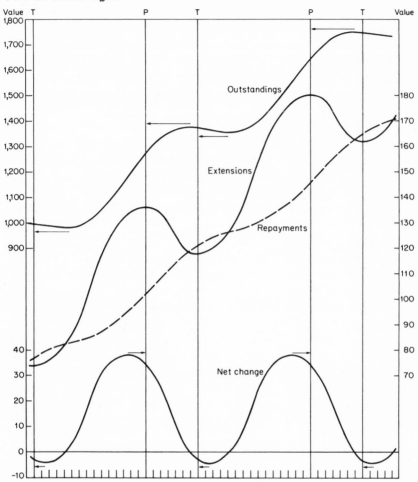

NOTE: *T* and *P* lines represent troughs and peaks in extensions.

produce a lead and the other (the trend effect) a lag. Hence, the leads tend to be longer at peaks. At troughs the evidence suggests that the cycle effect has been of greater quantitative importance than the trend effect because the net credit change has generally led extensions at troughs. The trend effect has been of greater importance in the postwar period than in the prewar period; hence, the difference between the turns at cycle troughs in net credit change and extensions has been smaller in the postwar period than before.

More generally, Part A of Chart 9 can help explain the customary pattern of turns indicated in Table 6. For the entire period the order of turning points at troughs is (1) net credit change, (2) extensions, (3) outstandings, and (4) repayments. In Chart 9, the point where extensions are smallest relative to repayments indicates the trough in net credit change (it is marked by a 1): the troughs in extensions and repayments can be read directly from the chart (they are numbered 2 and 4, respectively); and the trough in outstandings occurs where extensions and repayments cross (indicated by a 3). The order of turns (1, 2, 3, and 4) in the schematic drawing corresponds to the actual order found at troughs.[14] Clearly, the critical factors are the length of the lag in repayments behind extensions, and the rate of change in each. We might note that the timing relationships generally as between a series with no trend and one with trend will be affected significantly by whether the turning points are based on absolute changes, the procedure we have followed here and which the National Bureau has customarily followed, or on differences in rates of change.[15]

It should also be noted that we have found generally that the behavior of repayments has been determined primarily by its strongly rising trend since World War II. This is due partly, of course, to the absence of severe cyclical contractions in the postwar period. It should be remembered, however, that during unusually severe cyclical downturns both delinquencies and repossessions can have a potentially powerful effect on the recorded behavior of repayments, depending on how one measures repayments.[16]

In short, the timing relationships summarized in Table 6 are the logical result of a pattern of behavior involved in the process of

[14] The difference between repayments and outstandings is small historically reflecting the rising trend in repayments shown in Part B of Chart 9. The difference between the two in Part A is due entirely to the way they are plotted—middle of the month for repayments during the month, end of the month for outstandings.

[15] The latter is the method utilized by Ilse Mintz in selecting turning points in German business cycles since 1950. She employed this procedure because of the strong upward trend, and plans to extend the analysis to U.S. data. For a discussion of her method and her explanation for using it, see the *Forty-Eighth Annual Report of the National Bureau of Economic Research,* June 1968, pp. 77–79.

[16] In periods of severe contraction, repayments might be comparable to the entire change in debt outstanding in the event of repossession and subsequent resale, and may not change at all in the case of delinquencies. Thus repayments might still reflect considerable cyclical sensitivity in major downturns. See Philip A. Klein, *Financial Adjustments to Unemployment,* New York, NBER, 1965, especially pp. 13–15.

utilizing credit. The four series considered represent different facets of that pattern. Though net credit change may reflect the net effect on outstandings of the changes occurring both in the rate at which credit is extended and the rate at which it is repaid, it is well to remember that while extensions may appropriately be viewed as involving a bargain between the issuer and the borrower of credit, and so partially controllable by both, repayments are largely in the hands of the purchasers of credit. Indeed, repayments can be controlled by the issuer only indirectly—that is, on the basis of prior experience, which can tell him when and under what circumstances they are apt to falter; the actual individual decision to repay or not to repay is always out of his hands.[17] Otherwise, the issuer can affect repayments only by revising the obligation so as to extend the maturity.

What can be said of the possible impact of this pattern on economic stability? We have noted that, though net credit change leads impressively, it is a series about which none of the parties determining it make conscious decisions directly. Net credit change in fact reflects the difference between extensions and repayments. If one assumes that extensions increase consumer purchasing power and repayments diminish it, dollar for dollar, one might argue that the net stimulating effect of credit is measured by the difference between the two—i.e., by net credit change. Alternatively, one can argue that the net stimulating or depressing effect of credit on purchasing power cannot be properly measured by the difference between the two, but rather must involve the rate of change in each. That is, one can argue that the net impact of credit activity is stimulating only so long as extensions not only exceed repayments, but exceed them by more than previously so that net credit change will continue to increase (i.e., not reach a peak). An increase in the net credit change will cause purchasing power to rise, and a decrease will cause it to fall.

The latter view is similar to the argument about whether inventories may be said to stimulate the economy on balance only when they build at an increasing rate. The former is comparable to the view that any increase in inventories is stimulating. In this connection, Ruth P. Mack has recently observed, ". . . the levels of stocks on hand and on order, *and particularly the rates at which they change*, impinge on other aspects of the economy. . . and the manner in which they fluctuate." Again she has added, "Let me underscore again the im-

[17] See Geoffrey H. Moore and Philip A. Klein, *The Quality of Consumer Instalment Credit,* New York, NBER, 1967, for a more complete consideration of this problem.

portance of *rates of change*. . . . It means that the influences originate in what Arthur F. Burns has called the 'unseen cycle' of diffusion, in contrast to the 'seen cycle' in aggregates proper."[18] The peak in net credit change signifies, therefore, the end of the period of time in which the net effect of credit activity on the economy is stimulating; beyond this point in Chart 9, Part A, one sees the period of time during which credit outstanding, though still increasing, is increasing only at a decreasing rate.

In sum, at cyclical peaks since 1929, and especially since World War II, the net effect of instalment credit activity has been to reduce purchasing power for perhaps a year prior to business cycle peaks because there was a decrease in the rate of increase in extensions relative to the rate of increase in repayments, and that this change in the net impact of instalment credit preceded as well (also by about a year) an actual peak in extensions.

The causes for the change in the rate of increase in extensions relative to repayments are no doubt to be found in many factors. It is perhaps enough to suggest here that they occurred sufficiently in advance of business cycle peaks to justify placing them among the (many) factors precipitating the peak rather than among those simply reacting to the forces that develop as a result of cyclical peaks.[19]

[18] Ruth P. Mack, *Information, Expectations, and Inventory Fluctuations,* New York, National Bureau of Economic Research, 1967, p. 241 and 267. Italics added.

The correct measure of the stimulating effect of instalment credit has been the subject of considerable discussion and disagreement in the literature. In his 1942 study for the National Bureau, Gottfried Haberler argued that it was net change in credit outstanding itself that best measured the stimulating effect (see *Consumer Instalment Credit and Economic Fluctuations,* New York, 1942, pp. 140–141). More recently F. R. Oliver has taken the same position (see F. R. Oliver, *The Control of Hire Purchase,* London, 1961, p. 126). On the other hand, both Smith and Humphrey have argued as we do that it is the change in net change that is the best measure of the stimulating effect (see Don D. Humphrey, "Instalment Credit and Business Cycles" in *Consumer Instalment Credit: Conference on Regulation,* New York, National Bureau of Economic Research, 1957, Part II, Vol. 1, p. 20; and Paul F. Smith, "Multiplier Effects of Hire Purchase," *Economica,* Vol. XXXI, May 1964, p. 190).

[19] It is useful in connection with this argument to examine Charts 6 and 7. The reader's attention is called particularly to the decreased *relative* volatility in the cyclical movement of extensions, repayments, and outstandings in the postwar period. Net credit change (Chart 7) is measured not in relative but in absolute terms, and shows that the postwar period is much more volatile than the prewar

On the other hand, the lead in net credit change at business cycle troughs, particularly since the war, has not been very long though the differences in timing at troughs and at peaks are, as previously considered, largely a result of a rising trend. While the behavior of net credit change is less clear at troughs, there are nonetheless cases when it led by quite long periods. An increase in the net credit change series might well be influenced by whatever general forces are producing recovery in the economy. This is not to deny that the reversal in the net impact of instalment credit changes on the economy will not and does not strengthen and support the recovery, nor that it could play an important part on occasion. Rather it is to argue only that this reversal precedes (and hence perhaps helps precipitate) the recovery rather than accompanies it less consistently at troughs than at peaks. The line between initiating or precipitating factors in cyclical analysis and factors that accompany cyclical changes is a tenuous one at best. If economic activity and cyclical activity in particular tend indeed to be cumulative there must be factors that initiate such movement and it would appear appropriate to look for them among the leading rather than coincident series. The behavior in net credit change appears to fit these qualifications more clearly at peaks than at troughs, though it doubtless plays a relatively minor part.[20]

period (the former are charted on logarithmic paper, the latter on arithmetic). The changes in volatility must be interpreted against the great changes in absolute magnitude that characterize these series since 1929. Moreover, the great increase in volatility indicated in the postwar period for net credit change should be considered in light of our finding (Table 3) that although both credit and disposable income have grown greatly, the cyclical volatility of instalment credit is not visibly greater, relative to disposable income in the postwar period, than it was in the prewar period.

For a consideration of the prewar pattern alone, see Haberler, *op. cit.*

[20] In this connection, McCracken, Mao, and Fricke comment: "Great caution must be used in imputing to demonstrated leads a causal significance. . . . The broad conformity of credit cycles with those of general economic activity warrants the presumption that movements in consumer instalment credit do result in somewhat wider cyclical swings in business activity" (*op. cit.*, p. 56).

Conformity alone would not appear to justify such a presumption. Such a conclusion cannot be strongly supported by considering instalment credit in relation to business cycles in general. It requires an effort to relate credit to activity in the durable goods industry where it is used, which is the subject of the next chapter.

4

Automobile Credit

ONE CAN EXAMINE the impact on economic activity of changes in instalment credit more directly by confining attention to the largest single part of total instalment credit, automobile instalment credit. We have already noted that even relative to disposable personal income, which has itself grown greatly, automobile credit is even more important now than during the prewar period.

More importantly, however, one can carry the analysis of automobile credit farther than the analysis of total instalment credit, by relating the turning points in the various measures of auto credit not only to the business cycles but also to several measures of activity in the auto industry. This provides a more direct test of the hypothesis that net increases in credit may stimulate and net decreases depress economic activity.

We begin by examining the basic data. Chart 10 indicates in millions of dollars the pattern of changes of automobile credit extensions, repayments, and outstandings for 1929–67. (Net automobile credit change is charted separately and is shown in conjunction with related auto industry behavior in Chart 13.) A striking characteristic is the quantitative difference in the movement in all three measures of automobile instalment credit in the prewar as opposed to the postwar period. The critical role of extensions is revealed as well.

The *absolute* dollar changes involved in the cyclical movement of extensions and repayments in the thirties were a great deal smaller than during the postwar business cycles. Chart 10 shows clearly, however, that the *relative* volatility was much greater in the prewar period—that is, the cyclical changes represented a much larger per-

CHART 10

Automobile Instalment Credit Extended, Repaid, and Outstanding, 1929–67

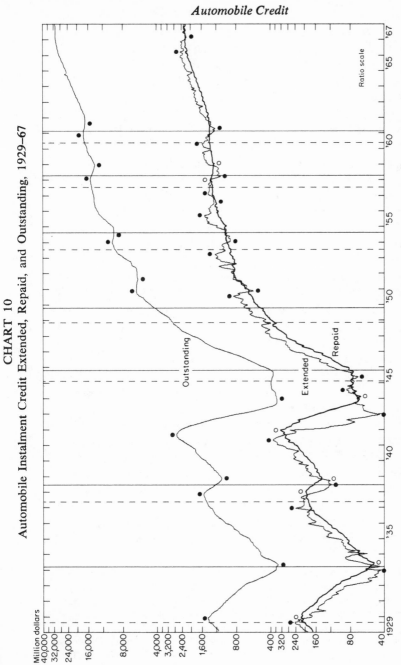

NOTE: Vertical broken lines represent business cycle peaks; vertical solid lines, troughs. Dots (outstanding and extended) or circles (repaid) identify peaks and troughs of specific cycles.

SOURCE: Board of Governors, Federal Reserve System.

centage of the credit outstanding during the 1930's.[1] Care must be taken in interpreting the chart on a dollar-for-dollar basis, therefore, because of the tremendous growth in automobile credit. Compare, however, the dollar decline in outstandings during 1929–33 with the corresponding decline during the mildest postwar recession (1953–54). The absolute dollar decline was far greater in the latter instance. Business cycles in the postwar period have been milder than either the 1929 or the 1937 recession. A comparison of the effect of the relatively sharp recession of 1937–38 on auto credit outstanding with the movement of outstandings during the recession of 1957–58 clearly shows in absolute dollar terms the much greater effect now of a mild recession on this series than in the earlier period.

The relative contribution made to the cycles in auto credit outstandings by extensions and repayments discussed earlier shows up in graphic form. Prior to World War II, the cycles in repayments seem, in dollar terms, almost as pronounced as they were in the extensions series. In the postwar period the cycles in credit extensions generally remain whereas in repayments they have almost died out, with the already noted result that it is fluctuations in extensions that now produce the cycles in outstandings.

A major reason for the postwar change in the cyclical relationship of auto extensions and repayments is the increasing length of maturities in the postwar period. In Chart 11, we have assumed that repayments in the thirties were spread over thirty-six months, as they have frequently been in the last two decades. The result of applying this assumption to extensions during the thirties is to smooth out the repayments series relative to the extensions, much as one finds actually to be the case in the postwar period. The net change in auto credit outstanding thus computed reflects the cycles produced by the fluctuations in extensions about the relatively smooth series showing repayments.[2] For all these reasons, the two cycles of the thirties, which would appear to be mild in absolute dollar terms, show up with

[1] The greater relative volatility can be seen by examining the percentage changes during cycle phases indicated for instalment credit in Table 3. The automobile sector exhibits a similar pattern. Chart 10 is charted logarithmically; when the series are charted arithmetically, the greater absolute volatility in the postwar period is very prominent, especially for extensions.

[2] The mathematics of this relationship, which in effect makes repayments a thirty-six month moving average of extensions (centered on the thirty-sixth month), has already been considered.

CHART 11

Automobile Credit Extended, Repaid, and Net Change in Outstanding,
Based on Repayments Estimated from 36-Month Moving Average
of Extensions, 1931–39

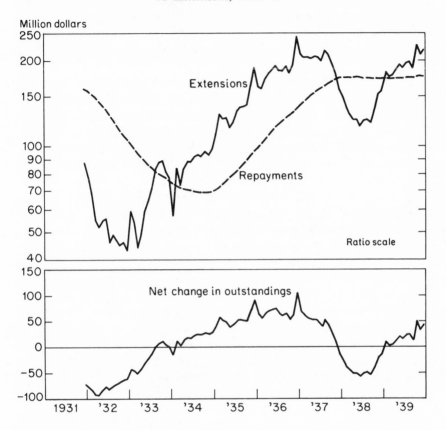

dramatic clarity in Chart 10. Indeed, Chart 11 suggests that the
1937–38 recession would not have shown up at all in repayments
had maturities been as long as they have been in recent years. The
Great Depression is still apparent in repayments. Thus the postwar
behavior of repayments is explainable in terms of the longer maturities
that have prevailed. But it is clear that the relative volatility in all
three series is greatly reduced in the postwar period. In this connection,
however, it is well to remember that these changes, though smaller
relative to the volume of credit outstanding, are still typically some-

what larger relative to the cyclical changes in disposable personal income.

The pattern exhibited by automobile credit alone is, not surprisingly, very similar to that of total instalment credit except that auto credit appears to be even more sensitive to cyclical fluctuations. The logic of the pattern is, of course, identical. Our principal concern here is to present the evidence so that we may subsequently relate it to activity in the automobile industry.

The pattern of turns in auto credit (Table 7) shows that generally net change in auto credit outstanding turns first and leads reference turns; extensions turn next, customarily with a slight lead; while repayments and outstandings turn last and with a lag. A careful examination of Table 7 will reveal that the degree of variability about the average is no greater and frequently smaller than with total instalment credit. In this connection, however, columns 1 and 2, which are based on the data underlying the relevant part of Chart 13 and deal with net change in automobile credit outstanding, show the importance of examining individual turning points and the degree of variability about the average timing, as well as the average leads or lags themselves. Examination of net change in auto credit outstanding as depicted in Chart 13 suggests that the trough in the 1929–33 recession leads by a longer period of time than for any other recession. We have suggested earlier, however, that there are good reasons why net credit change should turn with a longer lead at peaks than at troughs. While this also appears to be true in Table 7, it is less clearly so than in our consideration of total instalment credit and is not true at all for the two prewar recessions. The problem lies exclusively with the important 1929–33 recession, which, as Table 7 shows, was quite atypical.

Repayments fell sharply during the Great Depression, along with extensions. One of the two factors mentioned earlier in connection with Chart 9 as producing a longer lead in the net credit change series at the peak than at the trough, i.e., the "trend effect" so important in the postwar period, was absent in the thirties. We noted the importance of the rising pattern of repayments during the postwar period (the "trend effect") in the interrelationships among the turning points of the several measures of credit under review. Table 7 indicates how atypical was the timing of the turn for net credit change at the 1929 peak relative to the timing at the 1932 trough. Not only was there no "trend effect" but the fall in repayments was extremely large. This single episode was clearly a major reason for the failure of the prewar averages in the net credit change series to show a longer lead at peaks than at troughs.[3] Its importance is readily visible by comparing the prewar and postwar pattern of turns in net change in auto credit outstandings.

The average pattern shown by the sequence of turns in these four measures of automobile credit is summarized in Table 7. It is essentially the same pattern we found for total instalment credit. As with total instalment credit one must ask how regularly the sequence of turns indicated in the averages appears in the individual cycles. Examination of Table 7 shows that the order of turns was consistently present at every peak between 1929 and 1967 except that the 1948 cycle is visible only in net credit change. The order is therefore visible at the 1929, 1937, 1953, 1957, and 1960 peaks. At troughs, extensions and net credit change turn together at the 1958 and 1961 troughs, extensions turn before net credit change in 1954, and the 1949 trough is skipped altogether except for net credit change. Therefore, at troughs the pattern is somewhat weaker.

The economic implications of this pattern are, as with total instalment credit, the critical factor; the situation is comparable and the same reasoning may be introduced as a tentative hypothesis. The auto credit industry and potential borrowers together determine extensions. The auto purchasers who utilize credit determine directly the repayment record; the net credit change in outstandings is the result of both, and represents the net impact on the stream of expenditures being introduced into the economy by these two divergent sources. We would therefore argue that the net effect of auto credit has been to depress economic activity by a variable period but by at least something over seven months prior to peaks in the postwar period (though by a somewhat shorter period for the entire period because of the previously noted behavior of repayments in the prewar period). At troughs, the net effect of auto credit has, on the average, tended to stimulate economic activity slightly more than three months prior to postwar business cycle troughs.

Implicit in this argument is the assumption that when repayments do not take place on schedule, or fall in the aggregate (as in the prewar recessions), there is more total purchasing power available to

[3] Contrariwise, we may state simply that the presence of the "trend effect" in repayments may well be a major factor in the postwar period accounting for the longer lead in net credit change at peaks than at troughs.

Table 7

Timing Analysis, Auto Credit Outstanding, Extensions, Repayments, and Net Credit Change at Business Cycle Peaks and Troughs, 1929–67

Bus. Cycle Turn	Outstandings (1)	Lead (−) or Lag (+) (2)	Extensions (3)	Lead (−) or Lag (+) (4)	Repayments (5)	Lead (−) or Lag (+) (6)	Net Credit Change (7)	Lead (−) or Lag (+) (8)
				PART A: PEAKS				
8/29	11/29	+3½	8/29	0	12/29	+4	7/29	−1
5/37	10/37	+5½	12/36	−5	12/37	+7	12/35	−17
	8/41	—	4/41	—	12/41	—	4/41	—
2/45	NT	—	7/44	−7	NT	—	NT	—
11/48	NT	—	NT	—	NT	—	3/48	−8
	10/50	—	7/50	—	NT	—	7/50	—
7/53	12/53	+5½	3/53	−4	NT	—	12/52	−7
			9/55	—			3/55	−28
7/57	11/57	+4½	1/57	−6	12/57	+5	8/59	−9
5/60	11/60	+6½	4/60	−1	NT	—	7/65	—
			11/65	—				
			Prewar Period (1929–38)					
Average		+4.5 (2)		−2.5 (2)		+5.5 (2)		−9.0 (2)
Average deviation		1.0		2.5		1.5		8.0
			Postwar Period (1945–67)					
Average		+5.5 (3)		−3.7 (3)		+5.0 (1)		−13.0 (4)
Average deviation		0.7		1.8				7.5

Whole Period (1929–67) (continued — PEAKS)

	(1)	(2)	(3)	(4)
Average	+5.1 (5)	−3.2 (5)	+5.3 (3)	−11.7 (6)
Average deviation	0.9	2.2	1.1	7.2

PART B: TROUGHS

(1) date	(1)	(2) date	(2)	(3) date	(3)	(4) date	(4)
3/33	+1½	12/32	−3	5/33	+2	5/30	−34
6/38	+4½	6/38	0	11/38	+5	4/38	−2
10/43	—	12/42	—	2/44	—	4/42	—
NT	—	5/45	−5	NT	—	NT	—
NT	—	NT	—	NT	—	1/49	−9
7/51	—	11/50	—	NT	—	7/51	—
5/54	−2½	1/54	−7	1/59	+9	3/54	−5
11/58	+7½	7/56	—	NT	—	3/58	—
9/61	+7½	3/58	−1			4/61	−1
		4/61	+2			2/67	+2
		2/67	—				

Prewar Period (1929–38)

	(1)	(2)	(3)	(4)
Average	+3.0 (2)	−1.5 (2)	+3.5 (2)	−18.0 (2)
Average deviation	1.5	1.5	1.5	16.0

Postwar Period (1945–67)

	(1)	(2)	(3)	(4)
Average	+4.2 (3)	−2.8 (4)	+9.0 (1)	−3.2 (4)
Average deviation	4.4	3.2		3.5

Whole Period (1929–67)

	(1)	(2)	(3)	(4)
Average	+3.7 (5)	−2.3 (6)	+5.3 (3)	−8.2 (6)
Average deviation	3.4	2.7	2.4	8.9

NT = No turn.

NOTE: Leads and lags in months. The turn of February 1945 has been excluded from the averages for extensions for the whole period. Numbers in parentheses show the number of business cycle comparisons included in each average.

maintain or stimulate economic activity elsewhere and so, to this extent, falling repayments (rising delinquencies) can reduce the severity of a recession. In this sense, variations in the rate of repayments over the cycle can be viewed in part as an "automatic stabilizer." Since repayments, in the short run, are controllable by the consumer using credit, the consumer can partially offset income lost in recession by letting his repayments lapse. While he is thus delinquent, he continues to have the asset he is purchasing on credit quite as if he were making his regular payments, but his payments are freed by him for purchases elsewhere.

How long this can last is difficult to say, but repossession records suggest it cannot last longer, typically, than a few months. Recent recessions have been quite short, however. This reasoning must in any case be qualified. Rising repossessions presumably depress the credit industry; that is, cause them to reconsider their present loan terms to tighten loan conditions or to ease them less rapidly over time. Sharply rising repossessions could result, therefore, in lower extensions, while smaller increases in repossessions might simply reduce the rate of increase in extensions. Rising delinquencies, which can be viewed as postponing the effects of depression on the consumption problem of the consumers who resort to them, also herald to the credit industry that repossessions may soon necessarily increase—and so, as noted, depress the industry. The net effect of these forces on total economic activity is the ultimate determinant of the net effect repayment experience will have on economic activity. Finally, a full assessment of this net impact must necessarily consider the relationship of changes in the credit experience on the behavior of the consumer durable industry that it serves. This question is the major concern of the section to follow.

AUTOMOBILE CREDIT AND SALES

While the argument thus far has suggested that changes in auto credit outstanding, particularly in the prewar period when repayments fluctuated a good deal, could alter general purchasing power and so, in the very short run, make themselves felt in a wide area of the economy, it is clear that the over-all impact of auto credit, especially in the postwar period, must be initially on the automobile industry. If we are correct in assessing the effect of long leads in net change in auto credit outstanding, these effects should be visible in the activity of the auto industry.[4]

The basic data available for considering these relationships are to be found in Appendix Table B-1 and in Table 8, which indicate the turning points in series dealing with passenger car production and sales, and new passenger car registrations during the period 1929–64.

[4] There have been several recent studies of the demand for automobiles. Daniel B. Suits in his study, "The Demand for New Automobiles in the United States, 1929–1956," *Review of Economics and Statistics,* 1958, pp. 273–280, specifically included automobile credit as a factor influencing automobile demand. In his study for the National Bureau some years ago, *Factors Affecting the Demand for Consumer Instalment Sales Credit,* New York, NBER, 1952, Avram Kisselgoff included it as well. More recently Suits and Gordon R. Sparks in their contribution to the Brookings-SSRC quarterly econometric model attributed demand for automobiles to disposable income net of most transfer payments, the existing stock of new cars, "consumer attitudes and inclinations to buy," plus several other variables. They did not include credit terms in their equation because they believed it was subsumed under "intentions." That is to say, the ease with which credit can be obtained affects intentions to buy. Their equation was predictive rather than behavioral. (*The Brookings Quarterly Econometric Model of the United States,* edited by J. S. Duesenberry, G. Fromm, L. R. Klein, and E. Kuh, Chicago, Illinois, 1965; see particularly pp. 207–210.)

The University of Michigan model presently includes credit terms. Their estimate of the demand for automobiles (new and net used) is as follows:

$$\Delta A = \underset{(.033)}{.238} \Delta(Y - T) - \underset{(134.44)}{610.62} \Delta\left(\frac{1}{M}\right) + \underset{(.048)}{.281} \Delta\left(\frac{S_{t-1} + S_{t-2}}{2}\right) - \underset{(.065)}{.429} A_{t-1} - 2.434,$$
$$R^2 = .72$$

where Δ represents first differences in semiannual data; A = new and net used automobile demand; Y = disposable income; T = transfers; M = number of months to pay, average credit contract; and S = consumer savings. Lags represent six month periods. The absolute size of the coefficient on $\Delta(1/M)$ represents the small units in which the variable is measured. (Daniel B. Suits, private communication.)

Michael J. Hamburger has recently suggested that the purchases of consumer durables, including automobiles, are best viewed as investment, and as such are most affected by income, relative prices, and interest rates. He does not stress credit availability per se, although credit cost is obviously related to interest rates. ("Interest Rates and Demand for Consumer Durables," *American Economic Review,* December 1967.)

Finally, F. Thomas Juster has included the maturity on instalment credit contracts (though not downpayments) in the automobile demand model he has developed in connection with a study of the reliability of consumer anticipations surveys as a guide to consumer behavior. (*Consumer Anticipations Surveys: A Summary of U.S. Postwar Experience,* forthcoming paper to be published in the *Proceedings* of the 9th Annual CIRET Conference.)

Table 8

*Timing Analysis, New Passenger Car Registrations
at Business Cycle Peaks and Troughs, 1929–67*

	Peaks			Troughs	
Bus. Cycle Peak	New Passenger Car Registrations	Lead (−) or Lag (+)	Bus. Cycle Trough	New Passenger Car Registrations	Lead (−) or Lag (+)
8/29	7/29	− 1	3/33	3/33	0
5/37	8/37	+ 3	6/38	7/38	+1
2/45	5/41	− 4.5[a]	10/45	10/45	0
11/48	NT	−	10/49	NT	−
	8/50	−		8/52	−
7/53	NT		8/54	NT	−
7/57	9/55	−22	4/58	10/58	+6
5/60	NT	−	2/61	NT	−
	Prewar Period (1929–38)				
Average		+ 1.0			+0.5
Average deviation		2.0			0.5
	Postwar Period (1945–67)				
Average		−22.0			+3.0
Average deviation					3.0
	Whole Period (1929–67)				
Average		− 6.7			+1.8
Average deviation		10.2			2.2

[a]Excluded from the averages.

NT = No turn.

NOTE: Leads and lags in months.

SOURCE: Automobile Manufacturers' Association, *Automobile Facts and Figures,* selected issues, collected by R. L. Polk and Co. and used here by permission.

These turning points are derived from Chart 12, which presents the behavior of automobile production and registrations when available for the period 1921–67. It is clear that it is the New Passenger Car Registrations series that is most consistently available during the period for which credit data are available. New car registrations ought to conform closely to new car sales, given the legal requirement that all autos, when purchased, must be registered. New car production might differ to the extent that sales are made out of inventory or, contrariwise,

CHART 12

Automobile Production and New Passenger Car Registrations, 1921–67

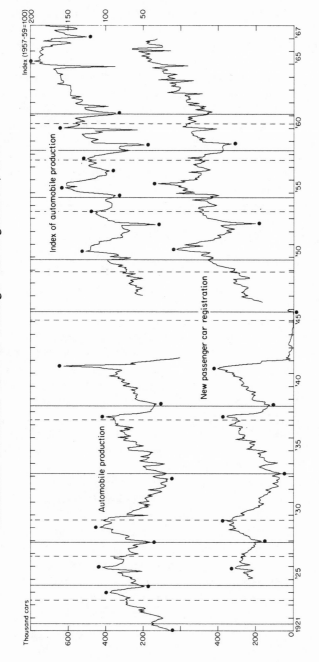

NOTE: Vertical broken lines represent business cycle peaks; vertical solid lines, troughs. Dots identify peaks and troughs of specific cycles. Production and sales are identical for the period 1921–34. For full information see Appendix A.
SOURCE: *Auto production*—Department of Commerce; *New passenger car registrations*—R. L. Polk and Company.

to the extent that production exceeds sales and so leads to a buildup in inventory.

What does the record show? First, it is clear that auto production declined in every business contraction after 1921 for which data are available. There was a slight tendency for production to lead at both peaks and troughs, though there are exceptions. Second, and most important, the behavior of auto production, auto registrations, and auto sales are closely related throughout. Indeed, in the postwar period the three series are more closely related to each other than they are to the business cycles. Production and sales are directly comparable only for the past few years, but they appear to be so closely geared to each other during this period that we have included only production in the chart. They turn in identical fashion during the last two business cycles.

In short, New Passenger Car Registrations seems to be a reasonably good proxy for activity in the auto industry, and in view of data limitations, we shall subsequently confine our attention to the relations between changes in the credit series and in new passenger car registrations.

An interesting aspect of the behavior of new passenger car registrations is a slight tendency to lead at reference peaks and to lag at troughs.[5] Thus, it would appear that declining auto activity may typically occur before a peak, but recovery does not usually become manifest until the general condition of the economy is picking up. That is to say, the contractions in registrations are generally longer than the contractions in business activity. One must remember, however, that the timing differences here are not numerous and are small, and there is, moreover, considerable variation.

The relationships among the turns in automobile credit, auto industry behavior, and general economic activity are presented in a schematic way in Chart 13 and in a more detailed form in Table 9.

Chart 13 shows all four measures of automobile credit as well as new auto registrations. It is instructive primarily because it shows that the general conformity of all these series to each other and to the business cycles was quite high during the two critical business cycles in the period 1929–41. During World War II, production activity was drastically curtailed in the automobile industry, terms of sale were controlled by Regulation W, and no cycles are visible. In the

---

[5] This is to be expected in a series, such as new passenger car registrations, that is not growing as fast as the economy (real GNP).

CHART 13

Chronology of Specific Cycles in Four Measures of Auto Credit and New Passenger Car Registrations and Production at Business Cycle Peaks and Troughs, 1929–67

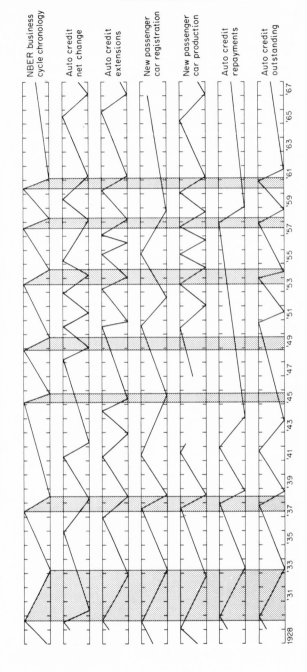

NOTE: Shaded areas represent business cycle contractions; white areas, expansions.

SOURCE: *Auto credit sales—Federal Reserve Bulletin*, selected issues; *Auto sales, registration—Automobile Facts and Figures* (NADA), selected issues, seasonally adjusted by NBER except January 1942 through June 1946; *Auto production—*U. S. Department of Commerce, seasonally adjusted by NBER.

Table 9

Leads and Lags in Two Measures of Auto Credit,
New Passenger Car Registrations, and Personal Income
at Business Cycle Peaks and Troughs, 1929–67

Bus. Cycle Peak	Peaks				Bus. Cycle Trough	Troughs			
	Auto Net Credit Change	Auto Credit Extensions	New Passenger Car Registrations	Personal Income		Auto Net Credit Change	Auto Credit Extensions	New Passenger Car Registrations	Personal Income
8/29	−1 (1½)	0 (3½)	−1 (1½)	0 (3½)	3/33	−34 (1)	−3 (2)	0 (3½)	0 (3½)
5/37	−17 (1)	−5 (2)	+3 (4)	+1 (3)	6/38	−2 (1)	0 (3)	+1 (4)	−1 (2)
2/45	NT	−7[a] (2)	−45[a] (2)	+4[a] (3)	10/45	NT	−5 (3)	0	−1
11/48	−8	NT	NT	−1	10/49	−9 (1)	NT	NT	−3
7/53	−7 (1)	−4 (2)	NT	+3 (3)	8/54	−5	−7	NT	−4
7/57	−28 (1)	−6 (3)	−22 (2)	+1 (4)	4/58	−1 (2½)	−1 (2½)	+6 (4)	−2 (1)
5/60	−9 (1)	−1 (2)	NT	NT	2/61	+2 (2½)	−1 (2½)	NT	NT

(Tie)

(continued)

Table 9 (concluded)

	Peaks					Troughs			
Bus. Cycle Peak	Auto Net Credit Change	Auto Credit Extensions	New Passenger Car Registrations	Personal Income	Bus. Cycle Trough	Auto Net Credit Change	Auto Credit Extensions	New Passenger Car Registrations	Personal Income
Averages									
Prewar	−9.0 (1)	−2.5 (2)	+1.0 (4)	+0.5 (3)		−18.0 (1)	−1.5 (2)	+0.5 (4)	−0.5 (3)
Postwar	−13.0 (2)	−3.7 (3)	−22.0[b] (1)	+1.0 (4)		−3.2 (1)	−2.8 (2)	+3.0 (4)	−2.5 (3)
Entire Period	−11.7 (1)	−3.2 (3)	−6.7 (2)	+0.8 (4)		−8.2 (1)	−2.3 (2)	+1.8 (4)	−1.8 (3)

aExcluded from the average.
bOne comparison.
NT = No turn.
NOTE: A − sign indicates a lead; a + sign, a lag. Numbers in parentheses indicate rank, where data permit. The initial turn in each group at each peak and trough gets a rank of 1, and so on.
SOURCE: Credit data—*Federal Reserve Bulletin*; new passenger car registrations—Automobile Manufacturers' Association, *Automobile Facts and Figures*, collected by R. L. Polk and Co. and used here by permission; personal income data—Barger and Klein, Department of Commerce estimates.

postwar period the situation is more complicated. Conformity to the business cycles is still present but less obvious, because it became increasingly clear that there were fluctuations present that were specific to the auto industry (or at least did not involve the entire economy). Moreover, these specific movements are present in all parts of the industry represented. Thus, the Korean War produced declines in three credit series (all except repayments) as well as in new car registrations, but was not associated with a general recession. On the other hand, the general recession of 1948–49 is reflected in none of the auto series except the most sensitive credit series, net credit change; for the rest, the industry was able to ride out the recession on the pent-up demand still being met from the war. The industry generally escaped the postwar readjustment cycle for the same reason. Similarly a set of circumstances unique to the auto industry produced a decline in 1956 in automobile extensions.[6]

In short, the auto industry and its associated credit industry appear frequently to reflect general recessions and so may be said to conform moderately well to the general business cycle. Having said this, however, it is necessary to add that all the aspects of the automobile sector included in Chart 13 would appear to show, in the form of extra cycles, that they are somewhat more volatile than the economy generally and that they respond with cycles of their own to factors that the general economy reacts to less severely if at all. Equally important, most aspects of the auto and auto credit industry move with a high degree of internal conformity.

While Chart 13 indicates the general state of conformity of these series to the business cycles, the details of the timing relationships among the turns at business cycle peaks and troughs, crucial in considering the possible link between changes in automobile credit and changes in auto industry activity, have been shown in Table 9. Table 9 should be viewed in connection with Table 10, which summarizes all the relevant information concerning the timing of automobile credit and automobile registrations that has previously been introduced. The

[6] It should be noted in passing that the auto credit series include credit utilized in the purchase of both new and used automobiles, whereas the registrations series refers *only* to *new* autos. Turning points in the volume of new and used automobiles have not diverged, although one might expect a shift toward used cars during recession and toward new auto purchases in expansion. If this is the case, it has not and need not logically affect the turning points (see Federal Reserve Board, *Consumer Instalment Credit,* Washington, D.C., 1957, for details of the patterns of turns for new and used autos).

Table 10

Summary of Timing, Automobile Credit and Related Auto Series
at Business Cycle Peaks and Troughs, 1929–67

Line	Number of Business Cycle Turns Covered (1)	Number of Leads (2)	Number of Rough Coincidences[a] (3)	Number of Lags (4)	Number of Timing Comparisons (5)	Number of Business Cycle Turns Skipped (6)	Number of Extra Specific Cycle Turns (7)	Median Lead (−) or Lag (+) PK (8)	TR (9)	Median Lead (−) or Lag (+) PK (10)	TR (11)	Average Deviation[b] PK (12)	TR (13)
1. Automobile Credit— Net Credit Change	1929–67	14	11	4 (0)	1	12	2	6	−8½	−3½	−11.7	−8.2	7	8.9
2. Automobile Credit Extensions	1929–67	14	9	6 (2)	1	12	2	8	−4[c]	−2	−3.2[c]	−2.3	2.2	2.7
3. New Passenger Car Registrations	1929–66	14	3	5 (2)	3	8	6	2	−1[c]	+½	−6.7	+1.8	10.2	2.2
4. Automobile Credit Outstanding[d]	1929–67	14	1	2 (0)	9	10	4	4	+5½	+4½	+5.1	+3.7	0.9	3.4
5. Automobile Credit Repayments	1929–67	14	0	1 (0)	6	6	8	2	+5	+5	+5.3	+5.3	1.1	2.4

[a]Rough coincidences include exact coincidences (shown in parentheses) and leads or lags of three months or less.
[b]Average deviations have been computed about the mean leads and lags reported in columns 10 and 11.
[c]Excludes the comparison with the February 1945 business cycle peak.
[d]End of month.
NOTE: Entries for averages and medians of different series are not strictly comparable because they cover different turns.
SOURCE: Credit series—Federal Reserve Board; new passenger car registrations—Automobile Manufacturers' Association, *Automobile Facts and Figures*, collected by R. L. Polk and Co. and used here by permission.

questions to which the pattern under consideration in Table 10 is relevant are of considerable importance. Does a major industry such as the automobile industry tend to expand and contract its activities prior to turns in general economic activity and so possibly contribute to their initiation, or does it tend to react to prior turns in economic activity and so merely intensify them? Further, what is the role of credit? Does it expand and contract before, at the same time, or after auto registrations?

The most obvious link between automobile credit and automobile industry activity here is suggested by extensions and new passenger car registrations. That is, extensions must show up almost immediately as new registrations because of the legal requirement that all newly purchased autos be registered with the state bureau of motor vehicles. If credit is indeed a determinant of auto industry activity, extensions might lead registrations (though it might be a determinant and not lead).[7] Table 9 suggests some support for this hypothesis but also that the issue cannot be resolved easily. Viewing the evidence as a whole, extensions lead registrations more often at troughs (all five times) than at peaks (three of five times). Taking all the turns covered there are eight leads, one lag, and one exact coincidence. Table 10 suggests that these leads at peaks and troughs are present, for median timing comparisons, as well as the mean comparisons shown in Table 9.

A comparison of the timing of the turns in auto credit extensions using the registrations themselves as the reference chronology clarifies some of these relations (see Appendix Table B-3). It is clear then that the relation between auto credit extensions and registrations summarized above has been fairly consistent throughout the period under review. Extensions lead in the two troughs in registrations prior to World War II as well as the three comparable troughs since. They lagged registrations in the first prewar peak and at the last postwar peak they turned together. Otherwise, the lead at peaks has been consistent but small since the war. This suggests that in the years when credit was a large factor, it usually expanded well before the industry activity increased. The relation between auto credit extensions and industry activity is therefore more clearcut at troughs than it is at peaks, especially after World War II. On the other hand, the tendency of the turning points in net change in automobile credit outstanding to lead at both business

---

[7] Moreover, as we have stressed previously, a lead in a series such as extensions can be no more than presumptive evidence of its being a determinant of registrations.

cycle peaks and troughs has already been clearly indicated. Assuming that the net stimulating or depressing effect of credit on industry activity is also relevant to answering the questions previously posed, it is appropriate to determine the relationship between turns in net change in auto credit oustanding and the behavior of the automobile industry. It seems logical to suppose that net credit expansion could stimulate and contraction depress sales, but by how much and after how long an interval of time one cannot say a priori.

We assumed initially that the turns in the credit series might first affect activity in the auto industry, here measured by registrations, which might in turn directly affect general economic activity. We have chosen to measure the latter by personal income (although obviously income must affect sales also). This line of reasoning leads one to expect the series involved to turn as follows: after a turn in net automobile credit outstanding, new passenger car registrations would turn next followed by personal income and the business cycle turn. (The length of time between the net change series turns and the turn in extensions depends, of course, on the behavior of repayments.)

Table 9, despite the ambiguities of the extensions-registrations relationship already mentioned, shows that it is possible to find a pattern in the leads and lags that is suggestive. Because of the importance of this pattern, the table shows not only the average timing at business cycle peaks and troughs, but the actual leads and lags on which the averages are based. Clearly the number of comparisons over the entire period (not to say during the pre- and postwar periods) is still too small to reach clear-cut conclusions, but we are also reminded that auto credit as a force of size and impact in the economy is still very new, and as such its behavior at cyclical turns is of increasing interest. Table 10 covers the behavior of credit over all the cycles during which it has been of significant size.

It is clear that net credit change turned down prior to new passenger car registrations at every peak for which we can make comparisons except (significantly) 1929.[8] It led not only the business cycle peak but (except in 1929) all the noncredit series included. Thus, one can

---

[8] The behavior of the two credit series, vis á vis new passenger car registrations, is less clear in 1929 than subsequently. It is possible, however, that given the relatively small size of total auto credit in the economy in the early period, movements in credit affected the auto industry less strongly then. In this case the less obvious relationship between them visible in Table 10 for this period might not be surprising.

argue that the decline in the net impact of credit might conceivably contribute subsequently to declines in auto sales (or registrations). All these series turn typically with leads and thus can be viewed as restraining influences setting in before the business cycle peak. Only personal income turns after the peak. One cannot show that the earlier influences are contributory factors to this decline, but the evidence is consistent with such a hypothesis.

The evidence for the peaks shows, therefore, that for the postwar period at least (when credit outstanding was large) net credit change turned down first and with a large lead, while industry activity as measured by registrations turned down several months later but usually also with a lead, and personal income turned down last and with a lag. However, only one turn in registrations has proved comparable since the war.[9]

At troughs the role of credit is also difficult to assess. Net credit change still turns (up) first in all the averages (though there are exceptions in the postwar period). Auto extensions, as noted earlier, appear to turn prior to turns in the auto industry with greater regularity than was the case at peaks. Our measure of auto industry activity turns later—and indeed the evidence suggests that registrations may lag at the trough. But at troughs personal income turns up early. Thus, by the time the industry reacts, both net credit change and personal income have risen. Both factors would tend to strengthen the demand for automobiles; indeed, net credit change and personal incomes are only two of the many forces that have turned up prior to the activity of the auto industry. The lags are generally not long, but their existence suggests that an improvement in the auto industry is

[9] In making timing comparisons such as these, it is clear the extra or skipped cycles can affect the pattern. We have, therefore, compared the turns in auto credit extended, outstanding, and net credit change to new passenger car registrations using the latter as the reference chronology. We have seen in Chart 13 that all measures of credit conform to new passenger car registrations more closely than to the business cycles, particularly for the postwar period. Appendix Tables B-2, B-3, and B-4 indicate the leads and lags for each of these three measures of automobile credit at turns in new passenger car registrations where such comparisons can be made since 1928. Appendix Table B-5 summarizes the average timing at peaks and troughs in new passenger car registrations of these three measures of auto credit. The averages confirm the impression given by the comparisons to the business cycles. The relationship of turns in credit to turns in new passenger car registrations is quite clear both in the prewar and the postwar periods. Net credit change turns before registrations, extensions also show a small lead, while outstandings turn after registrations.

not generally one of the prior factors that make recovery possible.[10]

To consider this question further, it is useful to examine Chart 14, which indicates new passenger car registrations, auto credit extensions, and net change in auto credit outstanding for the period 1929–67. It will also be possible with Chart 14 to consider further whether one can determine if turns in auto industry activity are more closely related to changes in auto credit extensions or to the more complex measure of net credit conditions reflected in net change in credit outstanding. Once again the relatively small variation in the change in net auto credit outstanding series in the prewar as opposed to the postwar period stands out. While the turns in the net credit series consistently lead the turns in the new passenger car registrations series (and both lead the business cycle turns), the general pattern of conformity of the two series is far less clear in the prewar period than it has been in the postwar period. There has always been considerable variation in new passenger car registrations over the cycle, though it has perhaps become more pronounced in the postwar period. But in the more recent period the relation of swings in registrations to swings in net credit change has become much more pronounced. The leads in the credit series over the auto series at both troughs and peaks continue to be prominent—if not always long (even during the two periods where there were no reference turns).

Chart 14 shows quite clearly how changes in auto credit subsequently are reflected in changes in automobile sales, both at peaks and at troughs. One cannot say if the effect is causal. The evidence is not inconsistent with the hypothesis that credit is a codeterminant of production and sales, here measured by registrations. The chart also shows how changes in auto sales in turn precede peaks in general economic activity.

---

[10] This statement needs to be qualified. One cannot adequately answer these questions with an analysis of turns. It is entirely possible that a decrease in the rate of decrease in auto production or sales could improve the general economic environment and so contribute to recovery.

CHART 14

New Passenger Car Registrations, Auto Credit Extensions, and Net Change in Auto Credit Outstanding, (monthly) 1929-67

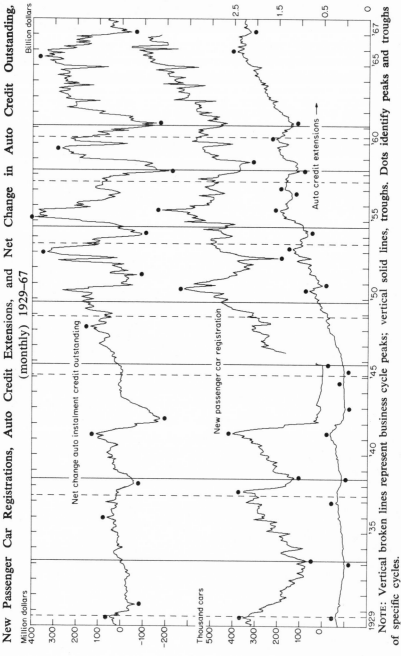

NOTE: Vertical broken lines represent business cycle peaks; vertical solid lines, troughs. Dots identify peaks and troughs of specific cycles.

SOURCE: *Auto credit*—Board of Governors, Federal Reserve System; *New passenger car registrations*—R. L. Polk and Company, used here by permission.

5

Conclusions

1. BOTH TOTAL CONSUMER credit and its major component, instalment credit, have fluctuated much more widely during the period covered, on a year to year basis, than has aggregate economic activity in the United States, as measured by GNP. Instalment credit has fluctuated more widely than noninstalment credit. While the credit series have had greater percentage increases than GNP during expansions and greater percentage declines than GNP during contractions, the differences have been greater during expansions. Credit has been growing at a faster rate than GNP during the period of this study.

2. We have examined automobile credit, the major component of instalment credit, in relation to disposable personal income and have shown that this relationship has been especially marked in the case of auto credit when related to the component of GNP most relevant to its immediate economic future. Both disposable personal income and automobile credit have grown rapidly in the years since 1920 but it is clear that auto credit, whether measured in terms of outstandings, extensions, or repayments, is a larger percentage of disposable personal income today than it was prior to World War II. Auto credit outstanding has increased seventeenfold since 1929 in contrast to disposable personal income, which has increased only fivefold. The imposition of Regulation W drastically curbed the use of credit during World War II, but since that time auto credit outstanding at the end of each year has almost never fallen below four per cent of disposable personal income for the year.

3. Along with this absolute and relative growth in credit, both instalment credit and especially automobile credit have continued to re-

flect cyclical fluctuations highly correlated with those in GNP. The potential impact of fluctuations in credit on economic stability via factors that might impinge on the availability or cost of credit, particularly instalment credit, or on the continued ability and willingness of consumers to fulfill their credit obligations is therefore even greater today than in the prewar period.

4. All measures of consumer credit outstanding have conformed to general business cycles quite consistently but with a lag at both peaks and troughs. This applies with few exceptions to total consumer credit outstanding, instalment credit outstanding, automobile credit outstanding, and noninstalment credit outstanding. Total consumer credit outstanding and total noninstalment credit have not shown cyclical declines in the postwar period. In general, credit outstanding has lagged by about six months at business cycle peaks and three months at troughs, with considerable variation in the length of lag from one turn to the next.

5. The general conformity to the business cycle extends to the flow of credit as well as to the outstandings. Thus, we find that net credit change and extensions (both for instalment credit and for automobile instalment credit) turn in close conformity to the business cycle turns. The exception is repayments, which generally ceased to exhibit cyclical declines in the postwar period.

6. It follows, therefore, that it is possible to compare the timing of the turning points for net credit change, extensions, repayments, and outstandings for both instalment credit and for automobile credit alone with the peaks and troughs in business cycles. The results of such a comparison reveal a distinct and logical pattern. Net credit change leads the business cycle turns, followed by extensions, which generally turn at or shortly before business cycle turns, with outstandings and repayments turning last and lagging business cycle turns. This sequence has been quite consistent throughout the period under review. It is logical because when a lagging series (repayments) is substracted from a coincident or leading series (extensions), the series representing the difference between the two, i.e., the net credit change, will tend to lead both at cycle turns. Repayments lag simply because the instalment method involves spreading the repayment over a period subsequent to the extension. Finally, credit outstanding lags behind the net change since it is the cumulation of net change, and it lags behind extensions for the same reason that the repayments do.

7. Automobile credit continues to be the largest part of instalment credit outstanding, and the most volatile part as well. It is also the only

portion that can be readily related statistically to the production and sale of the consumer goods for which it is utilized.[1] Moreover, because turns in auto industry activity can be compared to the business cycle turns it is possible to provide critical information relevant to the general assessment of the impact of credit on economic stability, as exemplified by the following questions. Does a major industry such as the automobile industry simply react to turns in economic activity and so merely intensify them, or does it expand and contract its activities prior to turns in general economic activity and become one of many determinants of business cycle turns? What role does credit play in all this? Does credit expand and contract in response to changes in the auto industry, or is the chain of causation the other way around? Unfortunately, the data do not yield definitive answers. Indeed, timing relationships can never provide definitive answers to questions of causality. They either are consistent or not consistent with hypotheses concerning causality.

We have argued that, though extensions are a measure of the most direct relationship between credit and the automobile industry's activity, net credit change is the best measure of the total impact of credit on consumer purchasing power at any given time; also that peaks represent the end of periods of increasing stimulation, whereas troughs represent the end of periods of increasing depression in so far as the impact on automobile purchases is concerned.

At peaks and at troughs we find that net change in auto credit outstanding turns first (and with a notably long lead at business cycle peaks), and automobile registrations turn later. It would appear, therefore, that changes in the net impact of auto credit activity, as measured by turns in net credit change, precede changes in the auto registrations at peaks. Registrations too, however, usually lead at peaks. At troughs the situation is more complicated. Both net change in auto credit outstanding and auto credit extended lead both business cycle turns and new car registrations, but the latter, in contrast to their behavior at peaks, lag more often than not at the troughs.

This suggests that the credit industry may ultimately play some role in determining the degree of stability that the automobile industry exhibits, and that this role is of great potentital importance in determining stability in the general economy. One cannot say how large a role on the evidence at hand. Net change in credit outstanding is simply one

[1] That is, we can compare the timing in the turns in auto credit activity with the turns in production and sale of automobiles. We have generally utilized new passenger car registrations as a proxy for auto production and sales.

of many factors that might precipitate subsequent turns in economic activity. The study of timing relationships provides insights into two critical areas—the relationship of automobile credit to activity in the auto industry, and the relationship of the auto industry to economic activity generally.

Our study is not inconsistent with the assumption that changes in the net impact of auto credit can make themselves felt in activity in the industry, both at peaks and at troughs. The evidence we have suggests that the auto industry may be more active in the precipitation of downturns than in recovery. In all these cases, however, it is impossible with the evidence at hand to be dogmatic about the conclusions reached, or to comment on the importance of the relationships that appear to be present, in comparison with the myriad other factors that help to precipitate both recessions and recovery.

Appendix A

A Note on Sources

Series	Source
New Passenger Car Registrations 1928–41, 1947–63	Automobile Manufacturers' Association *Automobile Facts and Figures* (Original source—R. L. Polk and Co.)
Automobile Production, Sales 1921–34, 1956–63	Automobile Manufacturers' Association *Automobile Facts and Figures*
Automobile Factory Sales 1934–41, 1946–63	Automobile Manufacturers' Association *Automobile Facts and Figures*
All Credit Series	1929–39, *Federal Reserve Bulletin*, June 1955. 1940–63, FRB, *Supplement to Banking and Monetary Statistics*, 1965. 1964– , *Federal Reserve Bulletin*, selected issues.

NOTE: There is considerable confusion concerning factory sales and auto production. The Automobile Manufacturers' series entitled New Car Production, 1921–34, is actually the same as that labelled "monthly passenger car factory sales," so that we have in effect a continuous series from 1921–41. The original source (*Automobile Facts and Figures*) carried regular footnotes explaining that what was called production in the period 1921–34 was really factory sales. Only the second half of their series labelled production (1956–63) genuinely represents production. Now they distinguish monthly production data defined as "the number of vehicles coming off the assembly line" from factory sales defined as "vehicles for which title has been transferred by manufacturers to dealers and consumers."

There need be no confusion about our use of these data. In Chart 12 the segment labelled production for 1921–34 represents sales as well. Only for the most recent period are the three measures of auto activity truly separable. However, in Chart 12 we have utilized Department of Commerce production data for the postwar period, rather than the Automobile Manufacturers' series because the former is available for 1946 to date, whereas the latter did not commence until 1953.

Table B-1

*Timing Analysis, New Passenger Car Production
at Business Cycle Peaks and Troughs, 1921–67*

	Peaks			Troughs	
Bus. Cycle Peak	New Passenger Car Production	Lead (−) or Lag (+)	Bus. Cycle Trough	New Passenger Car Production	Lead (−) or Lag (+)
	−	−	7/21	1/26	−6
5/23	12/23	+ 7	7/24	6/24	−1
10/26	12/25	−10	11/27	11/27	0
8/29	1/29	− 7	3/33	10/32	−5
5/37	8/37	+ 3	6/38	8/38	+2
2/45	7/41	−	10/45	−	−
11/48	NT	−	10/49	NT	−
	6/50	−		1/52	−
7/53	7/53	0	8/54	10/54	+2
	9/55	−		9/56	−
7/57	8/57	+ 1	4/58	9/58	+5
5/60	1/60	− 4	2/61	3/61	+1
	3/65	−		2/67	−

	Prewar Period (1921–39)			
Average	−1.8			−2.0
Average deviation	9.0			2.4

	Postwar Period (1945–67)			
Average	−1.5			+2.7
Average deviation	2.2			1.6

	Whole Period (1921–67)			
Average	−1.4			−0.2
Average deviation	4.8			2.8

NT = No turn.

NOTE: Leads and lags are in months. The data from 1921–41 are for factory sales; from April 1942–46 there are no data; and from 1948 to the present, the data are for auto production.

SOURCE: Automobile Manufacturers' Association, *Automobile Facts and Figures,* selected issues, collected by R. L. Polk and Co. and used here by permission.

Table B-2

*Net Change in Auto Credit Outstanding
and New Passenger Car Registrations, 1929–67*

New Passenger Car Registrations	Peaks		New Passenger Car Registrations	Troughs	
	Net Change in Auto Credit	Lead (−) or Lag (+)		Net Change in Auto Credit	Lead (−) or Lag (+)
7/29	7/29	0	3/33	5/30	−34
8/37	12/35	−20	7/38	4/38	− 3
5/41	4/41	− 1[a]	10/45	4/42	−42
	3/48			1/49	
8/50	7/50	− 1	8/52	7/51	−13
	12/52			3/54	
9/55	3/55	− 6			
			10/58	3/58	− 7
	8/59			4/61	
	7/65	—		2/67	—

	Prewar Period (1929–38)				
Average		−10.0			−18.5
Average deviation		10.0			15.5

	Postwar Period (1929–67)				
Average		− 3.5			−20.7
Average deviation		2.5			14.2

	Whole Period (1929–67)				
Average		− 6.8			−19.8
Average deviation		6.6			14.6

[a]Excluded from the averages.

NOTE: Leads and lags are in months.

SOURCE: New passenger car registrations–Automobile Manufacturers' Association, *Automobile Facts and Figures,* selected issues, collected by R. L. Polk and Co. and used here by permission; auto credit data–Board of Governors of the Federal Reserve System.

Table B-3
*Timing Analysis, Auto Credit Extensions
and New Passenger Car Registrations, 1929–67*

	Peaks			Troughs	
New Passenger Car Registrations	Auto Credit Extensions	Lead (−) or Lag (+)	New Passenger Car Registrations	Auto Credit Extensions	Lead (−) or Lag (+)
7/29	8/29	+1	3/33	12/32	− 3
8/37	12/36	−8	7/38	6/38	− 1
5/41	4/41	−1[a]		12/42	
	7/44	−	10/45	5/45	− 5
8/50	7/50	−1	8/52	11/50	−21
	3/53			1/54	
9/55	9/55	0		7/56	
	1/57		10/58	3/58	− 7
	4/60			4/61	
	11/65	−		2/67	−
	Prewar Period (1929–38)				
Average		−3.5			− 2.0
Average deviation		4.5			1.0
	Postwar Period (1945–67)				
Average		−0.5			−11.0
Average deviation		0.5			6.7
	Whole Period (1929–67)				
Average		−2.0			− 7.4
Average deviation		3.0			5.4

NOTE: For sources and notes, see Appendix Table B-2.

Table B-4
*Timing Analysis, Auto Credit Outstanding
and New Passenger Car Registrations, 1929–67*

Peaks			Troughs		
New Passenger Car Registrations	Auto Credit Outstanding	Lead (−) or Lag (+)	New Passenger Car Registrations	Auto Credit Outstanding	Lead (−) or Lag (+)
7/29	11/29	+ 4½	3/33	4/33	+ 1½
8/37	10/37	+ 2½	7/38	10/38	+3½
5/41	8/41	+ 3½[a]	10/45	10/43	−23½
8/50	10/50	+ 2½	8/52	7/51	−12½
	12/53			5/54	
9/55	11/57	+26½			
			10/58	11/58	+ 1½
	11/60			9/61	

	Prewar Period (1929–38)		
Average	+ 3.5		+ 2.5
Average deviation	1.0		1.0

	Postwar Period (1945–67)		
Average	+14.5		−11.5
Average deviation	12.0		8.7

	Whole Period (1929–67)		
Average	+ 9.0		− 5.9
Average deviation	8.8		9.7

NOTE: For sources and notes, see Appendix Table B-2. Auto credit outstanding is for the end of the month.

Table B-5

Summary of Average Timing at Peaks and Troughs of
Three Measures of Automobile Credit and New Passenger Car Registrations, 1929–67

	Peaks			Troughs		
	Net Change in Auto Credit Outstanding	Auto Credit Extensions	Auto Credit Outstanding	Net Change in Auto Credit Outstanding	Auto Credit Extensions	Auto Credit Outstanding
Prewar Period (1929–38)						
Average	−10.0	−3.5	+ 3.5	−18.5	− 2.0	+ 2.5
Average deviation	10.0	4.5	1.0	15.5	1.0	1.0
Order	1	2	3	1	2	3
Postwar Period (1945–67)						
Average	− 3.5	−0.5	+14.5	−20.7	−11.0	−11.5
Average deviation	2.5	0.5	12.0	14.2	6.7	8.7
Order	1	2	3	1	3	2
Whole Period (1929–67)						
Average	− 6.8	−2.0	+ 9.0	−19.8	− 7.4	− 5.9
Average deviation	6.6	3.0	8.8	14.6	5.4	9.7
Order	1	2	3	1	2	3

NOTE: See Appendix Tables B-2, B-3, and B-4. These average timing patterns are based on the 4 peaks and 5 troughs in new passenger car registrations as the reference dates. All three series show peaks and troughs comparable to those of passenger car registrations, plus additional turns not shown by registrations. Net credit has 8 extra turns (4 peaks and 4 troughs); extensions has 10 extra turns (5 peaks and 5 troughs); and outstanding has 4 extra turns (2 peaks and 2 troughs). The averages include 2 prewar and 2 postwar peaks; 2 prewar and 3 postwar troughs. The May 1941 peak has been excluded from all averages.

Table C-1

Instalment Credit Extensions, Seasonally Adjusted, 1929–67

(millions of dollars)

Year	Jan.	Feb.	Mar.	Apr.	May	June	July	Aug.	Sept.	Oct.	Nov.	Dec.	Total
1929	442	469	481	477	489	493	511	514	502	497	479	445	5799
1930	432	435	429	426	384	407	395	395	387	378	374	372	4814
1931	374	362	347	340	334	321	325	315	299	290	288	271	3866
1932	254	241	220	213	205	200	185	187	189	185	180	176	2435
1933	194	184	157	177	193	202	210	231	232	236	233	231	2480
1934	217	247	245	260	261	257	268	265	267	276	278	284	3125
1935	288	322	322	329	319	336	352	358	363	370	400	430	4189
1936	416	426	459	452	465	460	466	470	479	473	498	553	5617
1937	520	533	545	544	554	548	526	538	536	512	489	463	6308
1938	450	436	426	433	434	417	442	452	450	468	490	508	5406
1939	535	528	526	544	555	562	591	583	579	623	609	637	6872
1940	637	628	637	653	673	700	667	663	702	740	746	773	8219
1941	784	817	805	874	887	848	840	849	709	661	662	689	9425
1942	575	543	554	478	424	384	395	407	391	374	361	353	5239
1943	362	372	369	376	366	396	372	384	416	397	394	383	4587
1944	376	380	400	371	410	408	422	417	418	433	426	433	4894
1945	418	403	433	402	415	432	436	421	452	506	529	532	5379
1946	572	604	599	658	660	662	708	755	770	804	813	890	8495
1947	918	945	964	997	1000	1052	1031	1034	1098	1145	1264	1265	12713
1948	1256	1233	1308	1319	1302	1304	1336	1370	1381	1208	1263	1305	15585
1949	1262	1321	1393	1466	1548	1513	1506	1550	1532	1668	1692	1657	18108

(continued)

Table C-1 (concluded)

Year	Jan.	Feb.	Mar.	Apr.	May	June	July	Aug.	Sept.	Oct.	Nov.	Dec.	Total
1950	1674	1748	1726	1731	1788	1885	2086	1948	1983	1773	1543	1673	21558
1951	1853	1830	1797	1815	1819	1807	1846	2112	2144	2155	2207	2191	23576
1952	2210	2203	2168	2289	2561	2717	2533	2315	2456	2680	2600	2782	29514
1953	2716	2691	2883	2723	2627	2559	2610	2529	2541	2569	2609	2501	31558
1954	2409	2545	2420	2497	2449	2568	2578	2605	2624	2668	2776	2912	31051
1955	2940	3076	3260	3232	3275	3310	3247	3346	3403	3245	3254	3263	38851
1956	3289	3358	3300	3385	3290	3236	3283	3346	3268	3321	3450	3397	39923
1957	3454	3523	3492	3412	3529	3532	3579	3513	3519	3447	3486	3504	41990
1958	3442	3249	3225	3233	3219	3253	3295	3346	3288	3390	3490	3643	40073
1959	3758	3905	3815	3949	4025	3988	4098	4064	4195	4143	4018	3999	47957
1960	4147	4185	4183	4330	4148	4176	4174	4076	4160	3991	4025	3967	49562
1961	3879	3840	3928	3770	3917	4012	3960	4095	4052	4233	4268	4404	48358
1962	4278	4357	4418	4604	4644	4579	4640	4651	4543	4639	4855	4826	55034
1963	4899	4957	4973	5008	4985	5054	5164	5172	5181	5356	5074	5389	61212
1964	5366	5459	5567	5477	5676	5520	5670	5653	5792	5669	5623	5920	67392
1965	5947	6082	6107	6245	6167	6196	6383	6385	6434	6425	6530	6489	75390
1966	6544	6492	6673	6505	6472	6675	6732	6689	6578	6522	6657	6433	78972
1967	6501	6497	6510	6606	6554	6823	6776	6929	6973	6942	7032	7035	81178

NOTE: Seasonally adjusted by source.
SOURCE: Board of Governors of the Federal Reserve System.

Table C-2

Instalment Credit Repayments, Seasonally Adjusted, 1929–67

(millions of dollars)

Year	Jan.	Feb.	Mar.	Apr.	May	June	July	Aug.	Sept.	Oct.	Nov.	Dec.	Total
1929	427	420	422	426	434	447	455	458	477	462	456	466	5350
1930	462	467	468	462	450	457	432	436	419	407	410	408	5278
1931	397	390	396	378	374	361	360	364	344	332	337	313	4346
1932	311	299	289	285	277	259	258	243	235	234	216	215	3121
1933	211	198	187	193	189	191	200	199	203	212	212	218	2413
1934	219	221	219	233	238	237	246	242	247	243	246	251	2842
1935	247	256	260	262	269	274	277	284	300	304	309	324	3366
1936	330	342	355	364	383	395	396	410	414	416	438	445	4688
1937	453	462	469	481	508	496	496	504	510	519	511	507	5916
1938	479	508	477	485	487	471	480	464	467	474	464	474	5730
1939	477	474	464	491	477	502	515	515	519	521	536	569	6060
1940	552	558	561	586	588	595	608	596	629	642	636	657	7208
1941	671	674	717	699	722	748	748	763	767	767	783	795	8854
1942	772	766	749	737	720	686	670	680	626	610	582	560	8158
1943	554	539	518	502	487	470	447	439	432	423	410	396	5617
1944	409	393	398	397	404	395	404	405	407	420	411	411	4854
1945	412	416	410	417	411	415	422	416	428	441	452	453	5093
1946	473	486	505	515	531	546	571	582	612	631	637	696	6785
1947	688	718	761	779	795	852	862	869	942	932	987	1005	10190
1948	995	1012	1032	1053	1104	1135	1124	1172	1171	1144	1164	1178	13284
1949	1209	1207	1246	1247	1288	1290	1303	1320	1292	1344	1388	1380	15514

(continued)

Table C-2 (concluded)

Year	Jan.	Feb.	Mar.	Apr.	May	June	July	Aug.	Sept.	Oct.	Nov.	Dec.	Total
1950	1443	1461	1463	1466	1477	1493	1556	1575	1619	1629	1613	1650	18445
1951	1739	1764	1739	1856	1858	1855	1967	1962	2019	2081	2064	2081	22985
1952	2089	2033	2059	2057	2096	2143	2163	2100	2133	2144	2168	2220	25405
1953	2177	2251	2341	2324	2293	2323	2302	2350	2382	2379	2405	2429	27956
1954	2474	2532	2517	2469	2496	2546	2516	2581	2555	2547	2617	2638	30488
1955	2618	2658	2689	2712	2789	2785	2802	2857	2892	2955	2955	2909	33621
1956	2977	2970	2963	3083	3072	3056	3129	3105	3156	3146	3182	3225	37064
1957	3282	3262	3272	3249	3299	3314	3357	3332	3375	3330	3352	3453	39877
1958	3388	3383	3392	3345	3320	3353	3329	3378	3347	3362	3409	3367	40373
1959	3379	3477	3454	3480	3574	3501	3574	3575	3612	3621	3665	3711	42623
1960	3765	3700	3754	3858	3837	3851	3889	3840	3875	3891	3877	3864	46001
1961	3909	3914	3922	3944	3914	3987	3952	4011	3987	4064	4047	4072	47723
1962	4092	4097	4106	4119	4224	4190	4266	4263	4293	4271	4372	4341	50634
1963	4414	4462	4496	4487	4544	4568	4588	4620	4757	4793	4620	4835	55184
1964	4879	4889	4961	5009	5102	5052	5134	5154	5198	5198	5262	5302	61140
1965	5332	5485	5465	5500	5511	5601	5659	5729	5748	5805	5831	5855	67521
1966	5947	5954	6024	5974	5979	6126	6168	6087	6103	6142	6213	6112	72829
1967	6221	6281	6246	6393	6361	6531	6551	6585	6689	6631	6614	6652	77755

NOTE: Seasonally adjusted by source.
SOURCE: Board of Governors of the Federal Reserve System.

Table C-3
Total Instalment Credit Outstanding, Seasonally Adjusted, 1929–67
(millions of dollars, end of month)

Year	Jan.	Feb.	Mar.	Apr.	May	June	July	Aug.	Sept.	Oct.	Nov.	Dec.	Total
1929	2637	2654	2714	2792	2877	2956	3028	3075	3097	3127	3124	3104	35185
1930	3049	2991	2952	2937	2878	2849	2820	2779	2751	2724	2681	2653	34064
1931	2614	2579	2525	2487	2447	2409	2375	2325	2294	2260	2214	2174	28703
1932	2106	2014	1938	1881	1832	1790	1716	1665	1626	1584	1543	1516	21211
1933	1502	1510	1470	1434	1423	1426	1437	1475	1517	1544	1563	1549	17850
1934	1574	1603	1631	1653	1678	1698	1720	1744	1764	1800	1826	1834	20525
1935	1892	1964	2039	2102	2148	2201	2277	2345	2415	2473	2568	2636	27060
1936	2735	2826	2945	3037	3117	3184	3262	3310	3381	3422	3481	3555	38255
1937	3641	3721	3826	3871	3902	3946	3972	3994	4025	4018	4008	3940	46864
1938	3921	3808	3753	3714	3673	3638	3585	3576	3560	3552	3581	3676	44037
1939	3691	3735	3808	3844	3922	3988	4030	4084	4152	4250	4349	4450	48303
1940	4523	4574	4650	4735	4846	4958	5007	5072	5122	5200	5328	5465	59480
1941	5596	5800	5896	6028	6128	6178	6245	6298	6256	6150	6106	5972	72653
1942	5779	5594	5368	5116	4836	4541	4282	4023	3775	3525	3312	3047	53198
1943	2911	2746	2581	2456	2339	2270	2193	2142	2122	2093	2083	2056	27992
1944	2038	2007	2011	1984	1990	2011	2027	2039	2044	2056	2081	2094	24382
1945	2110	2084	2103	2080	2085	2111	2124	2128	2141	2208	2295	2370	25839
1946	2476	2560	2647	2790	2925	3049	3190	3366	3501	3670	3857	4015	38046
1947	4278	4462	4641	4849	5078	5286	5478	5662	5807	6002	6271	6444	64258
1948	6799	6996	7317	7630	7797	7910	8076	8252	8448	8503	8644	8811	95183
1949	8874	8981	9148	9393	9624	9796	9956	10198	10436	10729	11058	11352	119545

(continued)

Table C-3 (concluded)

Year	Jan.	Feb.	Mar.	Apr.	May	June	July	Aug.	Sept.	Oct.	Nov.	Dec.	Total
1950	11576	11835	12118	12384	12686	13043	13524	13920	14281	14411	14391	14401	158570
1951	14535	14614	14661	14613	14551	14451	14312	14492	14591	14665	14842	14979	175306
1952	15091	15243	15323	15545	16026	16605	16976	17174	17459	18018	18450	19004	200914
1953	19547	20000	20540	20970	21271	21488	21800	21948	22052	22258	22497	22532	256903
1954	22593	22683	22589	22660	22538	22524	22568	22537	22533	22632	22823	23083	271763
1955	23512	23930	24501	25021	25507	26032	26477	26966	27477	27767	28066	28420	313676
1956	28732	29120	29457	29759	29977	30157	30311	30552	30664	30839	31107	31279	361954
1957	31451	31712	31932	32095	32325	32543	32765	32946	33090	33207	33341	33392	390799
1958	33446	33312	33145	33033	32932	32832	32798	32766	32707	32735	32816	33092	395614
1959	33494	33922	34283	34752	35203	35690	36214	36832	37415	37937	38290	38578	432610
1960	38960	39445	39874	40346	40657	40982	41267	41503	41788	41888	42036	42139	490885
1961	42109	42035	42041	41867	41870	41895	41903	41987	42052	42221	42442	42774	505196
1962	42960	43220	43532	44017	44437	44826	45200	45588	45838	46206	46689	47174	539687
1963	47659	48154	48631	49152	49593	50079	50655	51207	51631	52194	52648	53202	604805
1964	53689	54259	54865	55333	55907	56375	56911	57410	58004	58475	58836	59454	679518
1965	60069	60666	61308	62053	62709	63304	64028	64684	65370	65990	66689	67323	764193
1966	67920	68458	69107	69638	70131	70680	71244	71846	72321	72701	73145	73466	850657
1967	73746	73962	74226	74439	74632	74924	75149	75493	75777	76088	76506	76889	901831

NOTE: Seasonally adjusted by NBER.
SOURCE: Board of Governors of the Federal Reserve System.

Table C-4

Instalment Credit Outstanding, Net Change, Seasonally Adjusted, 1929–67
(millions of dollars, end of month)

Year	Jan.	Feb.	Mar.	Apr.	May	June	July	Aug.	Sept.	Oct.	Nov.	Dec.	Total
1929	0	17	60	78	85	79	72	47	22	30	-3	-20	467
1930	-55	-58	-39	-15	-59	-29	-29	-41	-28	-27	-43	-28	-451
1931	-39	-35	-54	-38	-40	-38	-34	-50	-31	-34	-46	-40	-479
1932	-68	-92	-76	-57	-49	-42	-74	-51	-39	-42	-41	-27	-658
1933	-14	8	-40	-36	-11	3	11	38	42	27	19	-14	33
1934	25	29	28	22	25	20	22	24	20	36	26	8	285
1935	58	72	75	63	46	53	76	68	70	58	95	68	802
1936	99	91	119	92	80	67	78	48	71	41	59	74	919
1937	86	80	105	45	31	44	26	22	31	-7	-10	-68	385
1938	-19	-113	-55	-39	-41	-35	-53	-9	-16	-8	29	95	-264
1939	15	44	73	36	78	66	42	54	68	98	99	101	774
1940	73	51	76	85	111	112	49	65	50	78	128	137	1015
1941	131	204	96	132	100	50	67	53	-42	-106	-44	-134	507
1942	-193	-185	-226	-252	-280	-295	-259	-259	-248	-250	-213	-265	-2925
1943	-136	-165	-165	-125	-117	-69	-77	-51	-20	-29	-10	-27	-991
1944	-18	-31	4	-27	6	21	16	12	5	12	25	13	38
1945	16	-26	19	-23	5	26	13	4	13	67	87	75	276
1946	106	84	87	143	135	124	141	176	135	169	187	158	1645
1947	263	184	179	208	229	208	192	184	145	195	269	173	2429
1948	355	197	321	313	167	113	166	176	196	55	141	167	2367
1949	63	107	167	245	231	172	160	242	238	293	329	294	2541

(continued)

Table C-4 (concluded)

Year	Jan.	Feb.	Mar.	Apr.	May	June	July	Aug.	Sept.	Oct.	Nov.	Dec.	Total
1950	224	259	283	266	302	357	481	396	361	130	-20	10	3049
1951	134	79	47	-48	-62	-100	-139	180	99	74	177	137	578
1952	112	152	80	222	481	579	371	198	285	559	432	554	4025
1953	543	453	540	430	301	217	312	148	104	206	239	35	3528
1954	61	90	-94	71	-122	-14	44	-31	-4	99	191	260	551
1955	429	418	571	520	486	525	445	489	511	290	299	354	5337
1956	312	388	337	302	218	180	154	241	112	175	268	172	2859
1957	172	261	220	163	230	218	222	181	144	117	134	51	2113
1958	54	-134	-167	-112	-101	-100	-34	-32	-59	28	81	276	-300
1959	402	428	361	469	451	487	524	618	583	522	353	288	5486
1960	382	485	429	472	311	325	285	236	285	100	148	103	3561
1961	-30	-74	6	-174	3	25	8	84	65	169	221	332	635
1962	186	260	312	485	420	389	374	388	250	368	483	485	4400
1963	485	495	477	521	441	486	576	552	424	563	454	554	6028
1964	487	570	606	468	574	468	536	499	594	471	361	618	6252
1965	615	597	642	745	656	595	724	656	686	620	699	634	7869
1966	597	538	649	531	493	549	564	602	475	380	444	321	6143
1967	280	216	264	213	193	292	225	344	284	311	418	383	3423

NOTE: Seasonally adjusted by NBER.
SOURCE: Board of Governors of the Federal Reserve System.

Table C-5

Automobile Instalment Credit Extensions, Seasonally Adjusted, 1929–67

(millions of dollars)

Year	Jan.	Feb.	Mar.	Apr.	May	June	July	Aug.	Sept.	Oct.	Nov.	Dec.	Total
1929	189	202	210	214	221	220	243	245	221	231	211	177	2584
1930	173	184	178	173	133	158	154	154	149	142	136	135	1869
1931	131	124	116	117	114	102	107	103	96	92	92	88	1282
1932	78	68	55	52	55	56	46	49	47	45	46	43	640
1933	59	54	44	49	59	64	70	83	88	89	81	77	817
1934	57	84	73	84	89	88	92	93	92	96	93	98	1039
1935	110	130	125	126	116	122	134	137	138	140	164	188	1630
1936	162	160	173	180	186	192	184	183	191	180	193	242	2226
1937	209	205	205	204	207	206	199	216	210	193	180	159	2393
1938	149	135	130	124	124	118	124	125	121	134	153	157	1594
1939	183	176	178	186	194	188	196	197	187	226	209	218	2338
1940	239	251	239	245	250	248	235	227	249	290	296	317	3086
1941	348	348	357	379	373	362	335	308	265	242	237	269	3823
1942	151	126	117	88	80	73	77	86	70	57	53	44	1022
1943	50	56	61	61	62	62	60	69	74	68	69	70	762
1944	68	70	72	74	83	82	86	83	75	84	77	76	930
1945	74	74	79	71	68	78	79	76	86	97	106	111	999
1946	123	129	125	144	149	145	153	169	184	200	203	245	1969
1947	255	271	272	283	281	294	290	290	319	343	390	404	3692
1948	409	405	441	436	405	422	450	477	475	396	438	463	5217
1949	437	459	545	570	606	571	578	615	598	668	684	636	6967

(continued)

Table C-5 (concluded)

Year	Jan.	Feb.	Mar.	Apr.	May	June	July	Aug.	Sept.	Oct.	Nov.	Dec.	Total
1950	685	731	708	690	702	790	847	741	772	678	562	624	8530
1951	668	647	643	684	710	713	724	855	841	814	827	830	8956
1952	884	865	811	875	1052	1134	994	814	937	1090	1114	1194	11764
1953	1164	1177	1220	1161	1068	998	1049	1020	1034	1062	1054	974	12981
1954	897	899	902	937	905	1001	992	998	999	1016	1073	1188	11807
1955	1169	1290	1426	1373	1441	1459	1418	1492	1515	1376	1329	1363	16651
1956	1348	1390	1351	1321	1297	1250	1243	1265	1248	1251	1278	1299	15541
1957	1406	1405	1391	1366	1377	1377	1378	1342	1403	1357	1342	1316	16460
1958	1341	1191	1095	1162	1131	1135	1173	1165	1131	1159	1208	1402	14293
1959	1413	1463	1448	1507	1516	1522	1549	1507	1581	1538	1370	1332	17746
1960	1471	1548	1565	1596	1519	1504	1416	1446	1476	1358	1432	1315	17646
1961	1280	1226	1280	1219	1293	1343	1326	1348	1330	1410	1480	1470	16005
1962	1511	1553	1592	1645	1667	1638	1671	1691	1566	1700	1776	1739	19749
1963	1807	1809	1811	1870	1847	1820	1887	1845	1791	1948	1846	1975	22256
1964	1954	1996	1997	2014	2091	2019	2060	2074	2134	2014	1938	2160	24451
1965	2186	2249	2268	2299	2249	2285	2355	2372	2385	2338	2480	2443	27909
1966	2340	2340	2479	2302	2298	2419	2383	2431	2387	2378	2461	2297	28515
1967	2240	2177	2199	2217	2238	2338	2266	2285	2322	2321	2305	2306	27214

NOTE: Seasonally adjusted by source.
SOURCE: Board of Governors of the Federal Reserve System.

Table C-6

Automobile Instalment Credit Repayments, Seasonally Adjusted, 1929–67

(millions of dollars)

Year	Jan.	Feb.	Mar.	Apr.	May	June	July	Aug.	Sept.	Oct.	Nov.	Dec.	Total
1929	172	174	177	183	184	196	197	201	217	208	208	217	2334
1930	210	213	212	208	198	194	186	185	172	167	165	157	2267
1931	155	154	149	144	141	131	128	125	121	115	113	108	1584
1932	108	98	97	94	89	80	80	71	67	65	62	57	968
1933	59	54	54	52	49	50	54	57	57	63	63	57	680
1934	66	69	66	72	73	76	79	81	85	83	82	86	918
1935	86	89	92	94	98	102	104	107	118	116	119	127	1252
1936	128	132	138	141	146	150	157	165	167	167	179	176	1846
1937	181	184	182	186	188	186	190	197	192	193	195	197	2271
1938	194	192	184	181	176	165	165	154	151	142	141	144	1989
1939	151	151	151	159	155	158	164	164	167	168	172	180	1940
1940	184	189	190	199	204	207	211	215	221	228	231	233	2512
1941	246	247	280	268	273	294	294	286	308	302	309	329	3436
1942	293	292	262	260	249	224	219	228	196	184	172	159	2738
1943	144	133	126	111	102	95	84	79	74	68	67	66	1149
1944	70	64	72	73	77	70	76	78	76	80	77	75	888
1945	78	80	77	76	75	78	78	77	75	83	83	81	941
1946	93	98	102	104	111	115	118	123	133	142	139	165	1443
1947	166	172	190	211	205	221	239	236	260	269	287	293	2749
1948	286	297	305	321	335	355	349	380	385	351	373	386	4123
1949	396	396	421	424	443	449	449	466	461	491	520	514	5430

(continued)

Table C-6 (concluded)

Year	Jan.	Feb.	Mar.	Apr.	May	June	July	Aug.	Sept.	Oct.	Nov.	Dec.	Total
1950	536	552	565	557	572	574	583	594	621	624	611	622	7011
1951	670	669	664	715	729	724	791	802	796	842	827	829	9058
1952	860	822	820	815	837	850	873	793	829	824	818	862	10003
1953	842	865	903	916	882	893	887	917	937	929	947	961	10879
1954	967	986	990	975	963	994	971	1004	980	977	1014	1012	11833
1955	978	1006	1036	1041	1074	1091	1080	1131	1142	1152	1189	1148	13068
1956	1178	1188	1161	1231	1221	1190	1212	1204	1221	1243	1253	1248	14550
1957	1299	1286	1277	1279	1289	1286	1303	1275	1312	1305	1285	1348	15544
1958	1342	1313	1304	1316	1279	1276	1272	1278	1266	1263	1257	1273	15439
1959	1233	1290	1287	1276	1300	1283	1313	1297	1324	1303	1321	1355	15582
1960	1351	1335	1356	1365	1384	1378	1359	1376	1367	1386	1381	1356	16394
1961	1376	1368	1367	1370	1352	1379	1376	1377	1375	1389	1378	1377	16484
1962	1436	1408	1405	1397	1460	1435	1464	1480	1467	1494	1523	1509	17478
1963	1564	1566	1546	1585	1611	1588	1603	1610	1665	1686	1652	1721	19397
1964	1710	1736	1752	1786	1801	1783	1826	1830	1857	1840	1876	1898	21695
1965	1916	1947	1970	1975	1987	2007	2007	2068	2056	2080	2148	2107	24268
1966	2115	2135	2216	2145	2159	2211	2238	2223	2213	2244	2255	2225	26379
1967	2202	2217	2193	2235	2219	2281	2228	2240	2280	2301	2240	2250	26886

NOTE: Seasonally adjusted by source.
SOURCE: Board of Governors of the Federal Reserve System.

Table C-7

Automobile Instalment Credit Outstanding, Seasonally Adjusted, 1929–67

(millions of dollars, end of month)

Year	Jan.	Feb.	Mar.	Apr.	May	June	July	Aug.	Sept.	Oct.	Nov.	Dec.	Total
1929	1152	1180	1213	1244	1281	1305	1351	1395	1399	1422	1425	1385	15752
1930	1348	1319	1285	1250	1185	1149	1117	1086	1063	1038	1009	987	13836
1931	963	933	900	873	846	817	796	774	749	726	705	685	9767
1932	655	625	583	541	507	483	449	427	407	387	371	357	5792
1933	357	357	347	344	354	368	384	410	441	467	485	494	4808
1934	485	500	507	519	535	547	560	572	579	592	603	615	6614
1935	639	680	713	745	763	783	813	843	863	887	932	993	9654
1936	1027	1055	1090	1129	1169	1211	1238	1256	1280	1293	1307	1373	14428
1937	1401	1422	1445	1463	1482	1502	1511	1530	1548	1548	1533	1495	17880
1938	1450	1393	1339	1282	1230	1183	1142	1113	1083	1075	1087	1100	14477
1939	1132	1157	1184	1211	1250	1280	1312	1345	1365	1423	1460	1498	15617
1940	1553	1615	1664	1710	1756	1797	1821	1833	1861	1923	1988	2072	21593
1941	2174	2275	2352	2463	2563	2631	2672	2694	2651	2591	2519	2459	30044
1942	2317	2151	2006	1834	1665	1514	1372	1230	1104	977	858	743	17771
1943	649	572	507	457	417	384	360	350	350	350	352	356	5104
1944	354	360	360	361	367	379	389	394	393	397	397	398	4549
1945	394	388	390	385	378	378	379	378	389	403	426	456	4744
1946	486	517	540	580	618	648	683	729	780	838	902	982	8303
1947	1071	1170	1252	1324	1400	1473	1524	1578	1637	1711	1814	1925	17879
1948	2048	2156	2292	2407	2477	2544	2645	2742	2832	2877	2942	3019	30981
1949	3060	3123	3247	3393	3556	3678	3807	3956	4093	4270	4434	4556	45173

(continued)

Table C-7 (concluded)

Year	Jan.	Feb.	Mar.	Apr.	May	June	July	Aug.	Sept.	Oct.	Nov.	Dec.	Total
1950	4705	4884	5027	5160	5290	5506	5770	5917	6068	6122	6073	6075	66597
1951	6073	6051	6030	5999	5980	5969	5902	5955	6000	5972	5972	5973	71876
1952	5997	6040	6031	6091	6306	6590	6711	6732	6840	7106	7402	7734	79580
1953	8056	8368	8685	8930	9116	9221	9383	9486	9583	9716	9823	9836	110203
1954	9766	9679	9591	9553	9495	9502	9523	9517	9536	9575	9634	9810	115181
1955	10001	10285	10675	11007	11374	11742	12080	12441	12814	13038	13178	13393	142028
1956	13563	13765	13955	14045	14121	14181	14212	14273	14300	14308	14333	14384	169440
1957	14491	14610	14724	14811	14899	14990	15065	15132	15223	15275	15332	15300	179852
1958	15299	15177	14968	14814	14666	14525	14426	14313	14178	14074	14025	14154	174619
1959	14345	14518	14679	14910	15126	15365	15601	15868	16125	16360	16409	16386	185692
1960	16506	16719	16928	17159	17294	17420	17477	17547	17656	17628	17679	17638	207651
1961	17542	17400	17313	17162	17103	17067	17017	16988	16943	16964	17066	17159	205724
1962	17234	17379	17566	17814	18021	18224	18431	18642	18741	18947	19200	19430	219629
1963	19673	19916	20181	20466	20702	20934	21218	21453	21579	21841	22035	22289	252287
1964	22533	22793	23038	23266	23556	23792	24026	24270	25547	24721	24783	25045	287370
1965	25315	25617	25915	26239	26501	26779	27127	27431	27760	28018	28350	28686	323738
1966	28911	29116	29379	29536	29675	29883	30028	30236	30410	30544	30750	30822	359290
1967	30860	30820	30826	30808	30827	30884	30922	30967	31009	31029	31094	31150	371196

NOTE: Seasonally adjusted by NBER.
SOURCE: Board of Governors of the Federal Reserve System.

Table C-8
Automobile Instalment Credit Outstanding, Net Change, Seasonally Adjusted, 1929–67
(millions of dollars)

Year	Jan.	Feb.	Mar.	Apr.	May	June	July	Aug.	Sept.	Oct.	Nov.	Dec.	Total
1929	17	28	33	31	37	24	46	44	4	23	3	-40	250
1930	-37	-29	-34	-35	-65	-36	-32	-31	-23	-25	-29	-22	-398
1931	-24	-30	-33	-27	-27	-29	-21	-22	-25	-23	-21	-20	-302
1932	-30	-30	-42	-42	-34	-24	-34	-22	-20	-20	-16	-14	-328
1933	0	0	-10	-3	10	14	16	26	31	26	18	9	137
1934	-9	15	7	12	16	12	13	12	7	13	11	12	121
1935	24	41	33	32	18	20	30	30	20	24	45	61	378
1936	34	28	35	39	40	42	27	18	24	13	14	66	380
1937	28	21	23	18	19	20	9	19	18	0	-15	-38	122
1938	-45	-57	-54	-57	-52	-47	-41	-29	-30	-8	12	13	-395
1939	32	25	27	27	39	30	32	33	20	58	37	38	398
1940	55	62	49	46	46	41	24	12	28	62	65	84	574
1941	102	101	77	111	100	68	41	22	-43	-60	-72	-60	387
1942	-142	-166	-145	-172	-169	-151	-142	-142	-126	-127	-119	-115	-1716
1943	-94	-77	-65	-50	-40	-33	-24	-10	0	0	2	4	-387
1944	-2	6	0	1	6	12	10	5	-1	4	0	1	42
1945	-4	-6	2	-5	-7	0	1	-1	11	14	23	30	58
1946	30	31	23	40	38	30	35	46	51	58	64	80	526
1947	89	99	82	72	76	73	51	54	59	74	103	111	943
1948	123	108	136	115	70	67	101	97	90	45	65	77	1094
1949	41	63	124	146	163	122	129	149	137	177	164	122	1537

(continued)

Table C-8 (concluded)

Year	Jan.	Feb.	Mar.	Apr.	May	June	July	Aug.	Sept.	Oct.	Nov.	Dec.	Total
1950	149	179	143	133	130	216	264	147	151	54	-49	2	1519
1951	-2	-22	-21	-31	-19	-11	-67	53	45	-28	0	1	-102
1952	24	43	-9	60	215	284	121	21	108	266	296	332	1761
1953	322	312	317	245	186	105	162	103	97	133	107	13	2102
1954	-70	-87	-88	-38	-58	7	21	-6	19	39	59	176	-26
1955	191	284	390	332	367	368	338	361	373	224	140	215	3583
1956	170	202	190	90	76	60	31	61	27	8	25	51	991
1957	107	119	114	87	88	91	75	67	91	52	57	-32	916
1958	-1	-122	-209	-154	-148	-141	-99	-113	-135	-104	-49	129	-1146
1959	191	173	161	231	216	239	236	267	257	235	49	-23	2232
1960	120	213	209	231	135	126	57	70	109	-28	51	-41	1252
1961	-96	-142	-87	-151	-59	-36	-50	-29	-45	21	102	93	-479
1962	75	145	187	248	207	203	207	211	99	206	253	230	2271
1963	243	243	265	285	236	232	284	235	126	262	194	254	2859
1964	244	260	245	228	290	236	284	244	277	174	62	262	2756
1965	270	302	298	324	262	278	348	304	329	258	332	336	3641
1966	225	205	263	157	139	208	145	208	174	134	206	72	2136
1967	38	-40	6	-18	19	57	38	45	42	20	65	56	328

NOTE: Seasonally adjusted by NBER.
SOURCE: Board of Governors of the Federal Reserve System.

Table C-9

New Passenger Car Registrations, Seasonally Adjusted, 1925–66

(thousands of cars)

Year	Jan.	Feb.	Mar.	Apr.	May	June	July	Aug.	Sept.	Oct.	Nov.	Dec.	Total
1925	239	215	231	244	239	258	264	229	212	272	308	302	3013
1926	290	229	260	275	284	272	269	266	279	263	257	275	3219
1927	254	243	239	230	222	222	205	211	198	202	210	168	2604
1928	197	224	231	231	245	264	263	284	289	313	342	304	3187
1929	319	313	338	335	317	319	352	328	323	321	307	262	3834
1930	261	279	265	248	241	210	207	181	186	170	158	181	2587
1931	184	176	176	185	173	158	158	138	136	121	129	147	1881
1932	124	111	80	84	92	110	85	82	91	77	75	87	1098
1933	113	95	68	84	112	123	150	160	182	174	157	111	1529
1934	85	136	148	157	154	157	183	176	175	191	166	142	1870
1935	188	248	223	229	212	207	228	232	201	235	306	258	2767
1936	270	257	257	288	289	291	288	280	286	271	273	341	3391
1937	327	307	308	283	297	300	300	353	347	299	215	178	3514
1938	162	164	153	143	138	134	127	156	150	155	207	220	1909
1939	218	214	210	202	220	214	201	232	249	251	239	240	2690
1940	277	274	262	267	270	280	286	271	285	319	310	325	3426
1941	314	361	349	373	402	389	356	317	260	177	170	169	3637
1942	65	19	40	26	30	23	25	27	19	14	10	9	307
1943	10	11	26	27	25	20	19	18	15	14	12	9	206
1944	10	7	7	8	8	7	5	3	2	3	3	2	65

(continued)

Table C-9 (concluded)

Year	Jan.	Feb.	Mar.	Apr.	May	June	July	Aug.	Sept.	Oct.	Nov.	Dec.	Total
1945	2	2	1	1	1	1	0	3	3	0	32	26	72
1946	NA	NA	NA	NA	NA	NA	166	181	214	220	250	276	1307
1947	242	261	258	276	263	259	252	241	246	274	281	313	3166
1948	319	303	304	318	235	236	279	288	288	285	340	313	3510
1949	316	311	352	378	409	410	429	432	446	457	445	427	4812
1950	442	491	485	455	445	547	584	622	611	568	482	581	6313
1951	551	511	501	446	423	420	387	390	405	366	362	329	5091
1952	354	347	312	350	376	386	323	203	327	378	395	422	4173
1953	460	465	464	483	478	488	505	481	481	506	501	425	5737
1954	409	432	451	459	459	538	444	428	443	396	427	624	5510
1955	529	557	590	564	581	613	598	640	723	594	576	601	7166
1956	512	524	503	508	495	490	494	559	471	442	468	483	5949
1957	512	514	533	492	491	471	503	487	562	482	470	475	5992
1958	441	392	376	375	374	376	379	375	371	331	380	485	4655
1959	483	503	470	511	510	536	533	543	544	535	461	408	6037
1960	490	590	568	572	564	545	518	543	562	538	563	519	6572
1961	470	452	461	433	472	523	474	496	467	540	560	502	5850
1962	569	572	571	549	561	552	578	576	484	673	629	608	6922
1963	613	602	605	652	628	626	660	591	532	720	631	663	7523
1964	670	661	620	693	695	700	670	691	752	670	562	694	8078
1965	721	754	778	762	756	787	769	811	787	765	798	827	9315
1966	655	861	856	699	701	703	769	782	767	789	739	726	9047

NOTE: Seasonally adjusted by NBER.
SOURCE: R. L. Polk & Co.
NA = Data not available Jan.–June 1946.

Table C-10

Passenger Car Production, Seasonally Adjusted Data,
Factory Sales for 1921–42, FRB Index of Production for 1947–67

Year	Jan.	Feb.	Mar.	Apr.	May	June	July	Aug.	Sept.	Oct.	Nov.	Dec.	Total
						Thousands of cars							
1921	60.5	69.3	93.3	118.6	120.1	156.7	142.4	155.4	145.8	127.5	123.2	93.8	1406.6
1922	104.0	117.0	139.0	166.0	191.0	221.0	194.0	226.0	189.0	201.0	246.0	274.0	2268.0
1923	293.0	284.0	292.0	286.0	289.0	296.0	269.0	290.0	305.0	325.0	339.0	379.0	3647.0
1924	371.0	368.0	305.0	279.0	229.0	195.0	223.0	233.0	266.0	253.0	240.0	246.0	3208.0
1925	269.0	260.0	281.0	312.0	309.0	316.0	337.0	206.0	271.0	388.0	401.0	419.0	3769.0
1926	349.0	333.0	321.0	308.0	307.0	302.0	305.0	353.0	359.0	293.0	289.0	226.0	3745.0
1927	248.0	268.0	277.0	277.0	283.0	246.0	229.0	256.0	231.0	191.0	162.0	193.0	2861.0
1928	258.0	294.0	297.0	274.0	282.0	310.0	325.0	369.0	369.0	368.0	360.0	392.0	3898.0
1929	430.0	410.0	408.0	390.0	369.0	374.0	410.0	409.0	387.0	384.0	315.0	174.0	4460.0
1930	289.0	283.0	263.0	259.0	246.0	220.0	213.0	172.0	196.0	165.0	206.0	226.0	2738.0
1931	168.0	182.0	183.0	193.0	178.0	151.0	177.0	146.0	127.0	100.0	111.0	175.0	1891.0
1932	121.0	95.0	79.0	79.0	103.0	109.0	91.0	72.0	78.0	66.0	123.0	148.0	1164.0
1933	134.0	91.0	77.0	96.0	118.0	136.0	184.0	184.0	196.0	202.0	117.0	86.0	1621.0
1934	138.0	189.0	221.0	182.0	178.0	166.0	214.0	179.0	162.0	165.0	148.0	182.0	2124.0
1935	278.0	277.0	285.0	245.0	199.0	239.0	238.0	235.0	243.0	304.0	301.0	281.0	3125.0
1936	335.0	267.0	291.0	299.0	298.0	307.0	326.0	271.0	300.0	253.0	299.0	348.0	3594.0
1937	332.0	349.0	348.0	349.0	354.0	361.0	353.0	399.0	331.0	325.0	236.0	194.0	3931.0
1938	159.0	160.0	153.0	149.0	145.0	138.0	143.0	128.0	159.0	185.0	225.0	238.0	1982.0
1939	244.0	234.0	240.0	233.0	231.0	255.0	244.0	244.0	266.0	238.0	228.0	275.0	2932.0
1940	308.0	291.0	272.0	309.0	317.0	298.0	307.0	336.0	325.0	383.0	351.0	336.0	3833.0
1941	348.0	337.0	315.0	321.0	406.0	436.0	625.0	564.0	243.0	269.0	221.0	148.0	4233.0
1942	125.0	44.0	5.0										174.0

(continued)

Table C-10 (concluded)

Year	Jan.	Feb.	Mar.	Apr.	May	June	July	Aug.	Sept.	Oct.	Nov.	Dec.	Total
							1957–59 = 100						
1947	45.8	53.9	57.2	55.4	52.6	55.6	48.3	47.1	55.8	54.7	62.0	64.8	653.2
1948	61.8	58.4	62.7	56.3	46.1	57.5	68.1	63.0	56.0	73.1	68.1	68.4	739.5
1949	67.6	69.9	68.4	78.9	72.6	84.7	89.2	91.0	92.8	92.6	71.9	62.6	942.2
1950	90.1	78.3	80.6	86.3	101.0	122.0	115.4	115.5	115.6	114.9	114.5	109.8	1244.0
1951	103.9	103.4	104.5	91.6	88.6	87.0	73.1	73.7	75.5	74.2	73.7	66.4	1015.6
1952	63.5	64.8	71.3	73.6	74.0	74.4	29.3	46.2	83.3	85.1	92.6	93.7	851.8
1953	95.6	100.7	104.2	106.1	108.7	106.6	109.2	100.8	93.6	90.7	87.4	87.6	1191.2
1954	87.2	87.1	88.3	91.4	95.4	96.1	91.9	85.5	84.9	82.3	90.0	108.2	1088.3
1955	128.3	134.9	139.7	142.3	149.5	133.3	147.3	147.7	148.2	145.1	135.5	124.8	1676.6
1956	116.9	108.3	106.4	105.5	94.5	93.8	95.8	95.7	90.6	99.7	102.4	111.5	1221.1
1957	115.8	117.9	112.3	107.7	110.1	118.1	112.8	119.7	116.8	110.8	110.1	98.7	1350.8
1958	91.3	83.5	71.9	64.4	75.3	77.3	77.3	75.5	44.5	53.1	110.6	114.5	939.2
1959	111.4	104.8	114.1	121.2	123.6	125.3	127.2	108.9	99.3	109.7	53.7	98.1	1297.3
1960	150.9	140.6	132.0	130.1	133.9	135.4	122.8	127.9	133.2	136.6	122.6	108.2	1574.2
1961	89.4	83.0	82.4	103.6	113.5	121.4	122.9	123.7	91.8	114.4	131.5	136.1	1313.7
1962	129.1	126.7	126.0	133.9	140.8	128.1	142.4	142.3	142.0	142.1	141.1	141.3	1635.8
1963	142.6	142.0	141.8	141.9	144.3	159.9	151.5	151.3	153.3	154.8	155.1	155.6	1794.1
1964	155.3	156.5	152.5	160.0	160.3	161.7	162.6	165.0	146.0	83.0	145.1	174.7	1822.7
1965	182.8	178.9	190.7	181.8	183.2	183.8	182.7	182.0	178.1	181.1	182.5	182.4	2190.0
1966	180.3	177.8	180.5	178.9	166.0	167.8	151.5	141.7	148.6	177.8	166.7	167.3	2004.9
1967	141.3	120.5	136.5	149.6	149.9	156.0	160.7	163.7	133.4	135.3	144.5	175.1	1766.5

NOTE: Factory sales represent production.
SOURCE: Factory sales, U.S. Dept. of Commerce, Bureau of the Census, seasonally adjusted by NBER. Index of Production, Board of Governors of the Federal Reserve System, seasonally adjusted by source.

Table C-11
Total Consumer Credit Outstanding, Seasonally Adjusted, 1929–67
(millions of dollars, end of month)

Year	Jan.	Feb.	Mar.	Apr.	May	June	July	Aug.	Sept.	Oct.	Nov.	Dec.	Total
1929	5571	5642	5744	5849	5969	6064	6138	6201	6210	6229	6214	6190	72021
1930	6140	6106	6072	6037	5967	5909	5848	5786	5720	5655	5609	5542	70391
1931	5472	5425	5348	5277	5206	5119	5031	4932	4843	4751	4655	4574	60633
1932	4480	4391	4276	4138	4014	3899	3771	3676	3609	3538	3485	3433	46710
1933	3397	3364	3307	3260	3243	3235	3230	3262	3297	3324	3336	3357	39612
1934	3369	3402	3442	3486	3528	3560	3587	3616	3647	3692	3722	3770	42821
1935	3807	3876	3973	4090	4141	4229	4327	4391	4457	4527	4648	4747	51213
1936	4850	4954	5071	5204	5356	5427	5547	5614	5698	5784	5854	5931	65290
1937	6012	6106	6219	6290	6375	6446	6525	6585	6611	6616	6585	6464	76834
1938	6451	6392	6310	6225	6106	6032	5978	5974	5980	5980	6055	6122	73605
1939	6166	6248	6301	6333	6393	6451	6510	6594	6702	6809	6888	6971	78366
1940	7061	7104	7161	7263	7393	7528	7614	7725	7719	7812	7919	8040	90339
1941	8170	8303	8379	8640	8888	9044	9221	9385	9291	9130	8970	8829	106250
1942	8742	8560	8308	8019	7643	7241	6942	6664	6416	6192	5947	5745	86419
1943	5543	5402	5219	5107	4955	4871	4774	4702	4703	4710	4697	4692	59375
1944	4594	4561	4588	4588	4641	4676	4697	4724	4740	4763	4800	4880	56252
1945	4839	4808	4875	4812	4834	4896	4924	4935	4938	5073	5213	5400	59547
1946	5530	5723	5917	6177	6370	6518	6695	7010	7218	7466	7731	7988	80343
1947	8236	8516	8761	9038	9311	9518	9717	9924	10166	10444	10745	11059	115435
1948	11381	11651	11989	12325	12530	12755	13014	13246	13527	13593	13682	13794	153487
1949	13899	14019	14115	14416	14625	14850	15042	15344	15690	15975	16325	16612	180912

(continued)

Table C-11 (concluded)

Year	Jan.	Feb.	Mar.	Apr.	May	June	July	Aug.	Sept.	Oct.	Nov.	Dec.	Total
1950	16891	17212	17518	17891	18292	18763	19536	20121	20567	20617	20594	20582	228584
1951	21007	21244	21370	21230	21164	21068	20917	21177	21367	21474	21741	21820	255579
1952	21993	22265	22339	22625	23169	23775	24157	24455	24839	25416	25890	26491	287414
1953	27125	27522	28178	28591	28938	29108	29393	29685	29885	30098	30238	30275	349036
1954	30328	30352	30208	30290	30244	30286	30438	30437	30549	30729	30952	31355	366168
1955	31718	32209	32782	33365	33847	34512	34981	35625	36235	36636	37107	37564	416581
1956	37922	38317	38869	39054	39368	39594	39730	40021	40287	40475	40869	41017	475523
1957	41263	41564	41815	42056	42357	42571	42887	43130	43272	43413	43506	43640	511474
1958	43805	43630	43428	43298	43233	43120	43134	43155	43164	43298	43416	43854	520535
1959	44400	44834	45345	45804	46315	46932	47552	48195	48822	49427	49815	50147	567588
1960	50630	51247	51773	52495	52751	53155	53482	53679	54035	54259	54423	54567	636496
1961	54693	54725	54885	54607	54600	54676	54729	54897	55087	55355	55783	56231	660268
1962	56378	56692	57184	57794	58332	58798	59158	59627	59979	60462	61084	61637	707125
1963	62148	62663	63193	63766	64295	64804	65503	66240	66769	67452	68075	68824	783732
1964	69525	70221	70848	71383	72179	72883	73597	74140	74876	75482	75875	76693	877702
1965	77454	78215	78983	79921	80704	81535	82418	82968	83691	84503	85209	85983	981584
1966	86681	87433	88302	88876	89316	89814	90425	91188	91576	92002	92452	92806	1080871
1967	93132	93426	93794	93794	94165	94555	94877	95385	95817	96206	96752	97172	1139075

NOTE: Seasonally adjusted by NBER.
SOURCE: Board of Governors of the Federal Reserve System.

Table C-12
Total Noninstalment Credit Outstanding, Seasonally Adjusted, 1929–67
(millions of dollars, end of month)

Year	Jan.	Feb.	Mar.	Apr.	May	June	July	Aug.	Sept.	Oct.	Nov.	Dec.	Total
1929	2951	2984	3014	3044	3068	3087	3099	3110	3114	3123	3112	3109	36815
1930	3108	3098	3089	3078	3065	3046	3029	3010	2983	2957	2948	2908	36319
1931	2875	2844	2809	2776	2738	2697	2654	2605	2558	2511	2455	2408	31930
1932	2358	2310	2261	2211	2167	2125	2087	2052	2020	1987	1952	1931	25461
1933	1909	1883	1857	1834	1814	1795	1783	1777	1775	1776	1769	1788	21760
1934	1799	1807	1818	1835	1846	1857	1865	1874	1887	1891	1888	1919	22286
1935	1923	1935	1963	2005	1991	2020	2032	2027	2029	2038	2069	2090	24122
1936	2122	2151	2164	2192	2241	2236	2259	2275	2298	2337	2364	2363	27002
1937	2387	2423	2457	2461	2478	2492	2517	2545	2550	2556	2566	2508	29940
1938	2498	2491	2483	2475	2436	2441	2440	2444	2444	2433	2477	2477	29539
1939	2478	2518	2517	2500	2480	2477	2472	2484	2525	2526	2532	2540	30049
1940	2544	2532	2536	2532	2547	2572	2584	2599	2576	2588	2597	2640	30847
1941	2656	2655	2666	2712	2770	2807	2849	2901	2910	2884	2851	2884	33545
1942	2944	2917	2889	2860	2805	2732	2696	2672	2670	2682	2644	2634	33145
1943	2630	2647	2633	2638	2609	2612	2604	2580	2592	2615	2614	2585	31359
1944	2564	2557	2581	2598	2642	2674	2687	2698	2700	2701	2718	2742	31862
1945	2743	2730	2776	2728	2739	2791	2815	2823	2798	2858	2918	2987	33706
1946	3071	3170	3271	3379	3432	3475	3527	3671	3724	3791	3881	3919	42311
1947	3978	4050	4098	4147	4213	4236	4271	4314	4384	4461	4503	4554	51209
1948	4605	4645	4707	4761	4794	4863	4917	4947	4984	5026	5030	5055	58334
1949	5042	5021	4989	5065	5049	5063	5066	5110	5170	5211	5279	5348	61413

(continued)

The Cyclical Timing of Consumer Credit

Table C-12 (concluded)

Year	Jan.	Feb.	Mar.	Apr.	May	June	July	Aug.	Sept.	Oct.	Nov.	Dec.	Total
1950	5330	5349	5406	5521	5639	5724	6001	6167	6204	6187	6231	6262	70021
1951	6479	6613	6713	6606	6621	6619	6627	6680	6717	6806	6918	6855	80254
1952	6893	7022	7033	7077	7144	7183	7222	7275	7312	7369	7443	7490	86463
1953	7571	7531	7659	7666	7700	7656	7637	7708	7722	7762	7704	7729	92045
1954	7729	7696	7668	7740	7770	7808	7910	7878	7902	7983	8061	8192	94337
1955	8231	8330	8353	8444	8437	8569	8610	8702	8779	8885	9021	9150	103511
1956	9171	9184	9419	9365	9470	9547	9544	9594	9721	9698	9812	9814	114339
1957	9837	9892	9970	10048	10112	10139	10203	10285	10268	10245	10245	10309	121553
1958	10374	10285	10251	10255	10309	10325	10366	10448	10495	10581	10612	10709	125010
1959	10874	10955	11072	11085	11145	11232	11313	11357	11391	11453	11500	11505	134882
1960	11592	11729	11805	12045	12007	12076	12138	12134	12205	12291	12335	12380	144737
1961	12448	12470	12623	12545	12566	12636	12708	12833	12934	13009	13199	13305	153276
1962	13276	13314	13506	13646	13752	13811	13812	13929	14009	14091	14189	14252	165587
1963	14308	14358	14456	14496	14567	14589	14709	14922	15011	15093	15213	15389	177111
1964	15528	15660	15747	15837	16035	16212	16368	16473	16572	16691	16788	16928	194839
1965	17078	17229	17360	17489	17577	17776	17910	17905	17973	18159	18215	18309	212980
1966	18438	18563	18668	18769	18786	18771	18829	18952	18984	19048	19116	19107	226031
1967	19190	19205	19371	19370	19528	19658	19796	19908	20034	20103	20237	20214	236614

NOTE: Seasonally adjusted by NBER.
SOURCE: Board of Governors of the Federal Reserve System.

INDEX